# The Shape of Change

## On Leadership, Resilience, and the Urgent Art of Becoming More Human, Together

### Jennifer Brown

Copyright © 2025 by Jennifer Brown, LLC

All rights reserved. No part of this book may be reproduced in any form without written permission from the publisher or author, except as permitted by U.S. copyright law.

This book is for educational purposes only and does not provide professional advice. The authors and publisher disclaim any liability for errors, omissions, or outcomes related to the use of the information contained herein. Views expressed are solely those of the individuals involved and do not represent any agency or organization.

Printed in the United States of America

Library of Congress Control Number: 2025920458

ISBN: 978-1-969267-04-8 (paperback)
ISBN: 978-1-969267-05-5 (ebook)

Published by Twin Flames Studios

*To the seekers, the storytellers, and the change-makers, this is for you. May your leadership be guided by wisdom, resilience, and the unwavering belief that a better world is always possible.*

# CONTENTS

How to Read This Book . . . . . . . . . . . . . . . . . . . . . . . vii
Introduction . . . . . . . . . . . . . . . . . . . . . . . . . . . . . . . . ix

## Part 1: Facing What Is

UNCERTAINTY . . . . . . . . . . . . . . . . . . . . . . . . . . . . . 3
GRIEF . . . . . . . . . . . . . . . . . . . . . . . . . . . . . . . . . . . . . 9
STILLNESS . . . . . . . . . . . . . . . . . . . . . . . . . . . . . . . . 17
SURRENDER . . . . . . . . . . . . . . . . . . . . . . . . . . . . . . 21

## Part 2: Returning To What's True

TRUTH . . . . . . . . . . . . . . . . . . . . . . . . . . . . . . . . . . . 29
WISDOM . . . . . . . . . . . . . . . . . . . . . . . . . . . . . . . . . 36
COURAGE . . . . . . . . . . . . . . . . . . . . . . . . . . . . . . . 42
RESILIENCE . . . . . . . . . . . . . . . . . . . . . . . . . . . . . . 48

## Part 3: Opening With Care

BOUNDARIES . . . . . . . . . . . . . . . . . . . . . . . . . . . . 57
VULNERABILITY . . . . . . . . . . . . . . . . . . . . . . . . . 62

GRACE . . . . . . . . . . . . . . . . . . . . . . . . . . . . . . . . . . . . . .69
KINDNESS . . . . . . . . . . . . . . . . . . . . . . . . . . . . . . . . . .75

## Part 4: Relearning Connection

RESONANCE . . . . . . . . . . . . . . . . . . . . . . . . . . . . . . . .83
BRIDGING . . . . . . . . . . . . . . . . . . . . . . . . . . . . . . . . . .87
BELONGING . . . . . . . . . . . . . . . . . . . . . . . . . . . . . . . .92
CONNECTION . . . . . . . . . . . . . . . . . . . . . . . . . . . . .100

## Part 5: Emerging, Again

PURPOSE . . . . . . . . . . . . . . . . . . . . . . . . . . . . . . . . .109
POWER . . . . . . . . . . . . . . . . . . . . . . . . . . . . . . . . . . .116
INTEGRATION . . . . . . . . . . . . . . . . . . . . . . . . . . . .121
HOPE . . . . . . . . . . . . . . . . . . . . . . . . . . . . . . . . . . . .125

To My Readers . . . . . . . . . . . . . . . . . . . . . . . . . . . . .131
Stay in the Conversation . . . . . . . . . . . . . . . . . . . . . .133
Bring Me to Your Organization or Event . . . . . . . . . .135
About the Author . . . . . . . . . . . . . . . . . . . . . . . . . . .137

# HOW TO READ THIS BOOK

*not a manual, but a moment*

This book is an invitation, not an instruction.

It was born in conversation. Not just the words spoken on a podcast, but the pauses, the reckoning, the truth-telling that have long shaped The Will to Change. These pages carry the voices of those who have lived the complexity of change, who have unlearned, shed, and reimagined what inclusive leadership can truly mean.

You don't need to read it straight through. Let your curiosity guide you. Start where you feel called. Some passages may feel like fresh air. Others may stir discomfort. That's not a problem. It's part of the practice. Inclusion is not a destination but a daily choice, a way of being, a commitment to the work of becoming.

The language here may feel poetic or nonlinear. That's intentional. This isn't a how-to guide. It's a pause. A breath. A space to reconnect with the human side of change—yours, and ours.

This book emerged through layered, intentional collaboration. I'm deeply grateful to those who helped shape its voice and form, especially my team at Jennifer Brown Speaks and the Podcast Alchemy team, who saw this vision right from the beginning. We also partnered with generative AI tools in a human-led, values-rooted creative process. The result is a new kind of co-authorship. One that reflects what's possible when we stay curious, iterative, and open to emerging tools of expression.

This work lives at the edge of what's known—between the personal and the collective, the individual and the systemic. It reflects the liminal space we're in: one where identities shift, norms dissolve, and new ways of leading come into view. That shift asks something of each of us. It asks us to stay open, stay humble, and keep showing up.

You are part of that unfolding now. Bring your full self. Take what resonates. Leave space for what might become.

# INTRODUCTION

## *being changed*

We don't often change willingly or gracefully. Most of us resist it, especially when it's messy, incomprehensible, and not of our own choosing. We cling. We bargain. We try to preserve what feels familiar, even when it no longer fits.

And yet, here we are: in the thick of a change we didn't ask for, unmoored by endings that came too fast, clarity that hasn't arrived, and identities that no longer fit. We feel fractured. Disoriented. Tired. Like we're holding it together with string and breath and stubborn hope.

We are living through a threshold moment. A disruptive, divisive, volatile moment. Institutions are cracking under the pressure, communities are splintering along deepening fault lines, and many of us are struggling to maintain our footing on shifting ground. The familiar landscapes of work, leadership, and belonging have been irrevocably altered, leaving us to navigate territory for which we have no reliable maps.

And the more fiercely we resist that reality—the more tightly we grip the versions of ourselves or the world we once knew—the more brittle we become. It's a quiet unraveling disguised as control. But true evolution doesn't come through clinging. It comes through the willingness to loosen our grip. To allow what no longer fits to fall away.

## The Shape of Change

This book is about letting go. About finding the courage to surrender and the willingness to be transformed. It emerged from a set of questions I return to again and again as I navigate my own shifting realities:

- *How do we stay rooted when the ground is unstable?*
- *How do we lead when the path is unclear?*
- *How do we keep showing up—fully human—in times like these?*

There's a saying about change that most of us know well: "When one door closes, another one opens." And while there's a kind of beautiful optimism in that, it also reflects a deeper cultural discomfort. Because between the door of where we've been and the door to where we're going lies a hallway. A liminal space. One that's often dark, disorienting, and stripped of direction.

And as my friend and podcast producer Doug Foresta wisely points out about this saying, "Yeah, but it's hell in the hallway."

We laugh, but we know it's true. The hallway is uncomfortable by design. It's the space where certainty dissolves and clarity hasn't yet arrived. It's where we shed what no longer fits and begin, slowly and imperfectly, to shape what's next.

I've spent my career examining how organizations evolve and how humans navigate change. What I've observed is that we've become masters of pushing forward while ignoring the wisdom of cycles. We prize productivity over process. Constant growth over natural rhythms. Certainty over the generative potential of not knowing. We mistake resilience for an ability to endure, rather than a capacity to transform.

No wonder this current moment feels so disorienting. Our collective addiction to linear progress has left us unequipped

## Introduction

for the cyclical, composting nature of profound change. We stand in that hallway now, between what's crumbling and what has yet to take shape, and the old tools no longer serve us.

If we are to move forward—individually and collectively—we need to begin by reimagining what leadership means. Not as a title, role, or position of authority, but as a way of being in the world. A daily choice to move with humility and humanity. A practice of showing up, imperfectly but wholeheartedly, with a steady commitment to building the world we long for, even when the path ahead remains unclear.

This kind of leadership requires a different type of wisdom. Not just the kind taught in boardrooms and business schools, but the deeper knowing that lives in the body, in the margins, in spiritual spaces and sacred traditions. The kind encoded in our nervous systems, passed down through ancestral lineages, and whispered through the rhythms of the natural world—in the way the ocean recedes and returns, in the way fungi break down what no longer serves so something new can grow.

And we can't do it alone. We need to reclaim community, the kind Adrienne Rich spoke of when she wrote, "There must be those among whom we can sit down and weep, and still be counted as warriors."

> *There must be those among whom*
> *we can sit down and weep, and*
> *still be counted as warriors.*

This is the leadership our times demand: leadership that makes space for grief and truth-telling, for tenderness, rage, and recovery. Leadership that does not shrink from discomfort, but learns to breathe inside it. Leadership that burns, sometimes painfully, through old identities, false certainties, and inherited scripts, and rises from the ashes not polished, but forged. Like the mythical phoenix, not simply reborn, but remade.

This book is for those of us standing in the fire, trying to lead, live, and stay open-hearted in a world coming undone. A world moving through the volatile process of breaking and re-forming.

The essays you'll find in these pages don't offer neat solutions because there are none. Instead, they hold space for the truths beneath the ambiguity: belonging, courage, kindness, resilience, hope. They invite us to stay present through the unraveling, and to listen for what might be asking to emerge.

My prayer is that these reflections serve as a companion on your journey through endings and beginnings, through the quiet work of release and the slow unfolding of renewal. A reminder that grief is not linear, nor is it something we navigate alone. And that meaning can and will take root, even in the wake of profound loss.

I invite you to enter these pages not in search of answers, but in search of better questions.

To read not for a formula, but for resonance.

To come not for a manual, but for a mirror. A sacred space for your own becoming.

Because transformation doesn't come from clinging to what was, or from rushing toward what's next. It comes from standing still in the hallway. From letting the illusions fall away. From allowing ourselves to dissolve gently and bravely into the deeper truths that remain when everything else has broken open.

# Introduction

*Transformation doesn't come from clinging to what was, or from rushing toward what's next. It comes from standing still.*

This is how we build real resilience, not by hardening, but by softening into what is true. It's how we emerge, not untouched, but unmistakably changed.

Scarred, perhaps. But more whole. More true. More good. More beautiful.

Welcome to the hallway. The liminal space where the old unravels and the new begins. Let's walk together toward whatever comes next, with courage enough to be changed.

# PART 1
## Facing What Is

# UNCERTAINTY

## *facing our VUCA/BANI world*

I sometimes wonder if any of us truly understand the landscape we're traversing. We use terms like "unprecedented" and "turbulent" so frequently they've almost lost their meaning, yet they remain accurate descriptors for our times. We're navigating a world that business strategists call VUCA—Volatile, Uncertain, Complex, and Ambiguous—layered with what futurists have called BANI—Brittle, Anxious, Nonlinear, and Incomprehensible.

Our human systems—social, economic, and organizational—weren't built for the level of uncertainty we're experiencing today. Modern society has been designed to minimize unpredictability, to insulate us from chaos, to promise control. We've built linear systems that reward certainty and clarity, that seek to manage complexity rather than move with it. But the truth is, uncertainty is not new; it's only our capacity to tolerate it that has atrophied. Our ancestors likely understood this better than we do. They lived in deeper relationship with nature's rhythms, with cycles of growth, decay, and regeneration.

Reclaiming our ancestral resilience—remembering how to move through uncertainty rather than against it—has become one of the most vital leadership practices of our time.

And perhaps the most counterintuitive part of that practice is this: it starts not with action, but with acknowledgement. Naming the uncertainty. Sitting with it. Letting it teach us. Even embracing it. There's a quote from Ram Dass that I've returned to repeatedly during these uncertain times: "I've been asked many times whether this is the Aquarian age and it's all just beginning, or if this is Armageddon and this is the end. And I have to admit, I don't know. Whichever way it goes, my work is the same. My work is to quiet my mind and open my heart and relieve suffering wherever I find it."

> **Perhaps the most counterintuitive part of managing uncertainty is this: it starts not with action, but with acknowledgement.**

I've thought about these words in boardrooms and on stages, in moments when I felt the weight of an audience's expectations. They remind me that leadership isn't about having all the answers; it's about maintaining purpose and humanity when answers are elusive.

In our work with organizations, this reframing of what leadership means has become central. The old paradigm—the all-knowing, directive leader who maps the certain path forward—can't withstand our VUCA/BANI reality. Instead, I see a new kind of leader emerging: the person who can acknowledge uncertainty while maintaining core values, who can say, *"I don't know what's ahead, but I know how we'll face it together."*

This human-to-human connection becomes our compass when traditional maps fail us. It's why, despite all the uncertainty, I remain fundamentally optimistic about our capacity to navigate this landscape, not because I believe the world is becoming less complex or volatile, but because I believe in our ability to evolve *how* we move through it.

There's a beautiful passage from Rebecca Solnit that captures this: "They want you to feel powerless and to surrender and to let them trample everything. And you're not going to let them. You're not giving up, and neither am I. You may need to grieve or scream or take time off, but you have a role no matter what. And right now, good friends and good principles are worth gathering in. Remember what you love and remember what loves you." She continues, "There is no alternative to persevering, and that does not require you to feel good. You can walk on in the rain."

Walking on in the rain. That image resonates deeply with me because it acknowledges both the discomfort and the forward motion. We don't need to wait for the storm to pass. We need to learn to walk in and even dance with the rain.

Perhaps most importantly, we need to recognize that uncertainty doesn't eliminate our capacity for impact; it simply changes the nature of how that impact manifests. As I often say to leaders struggling with the ambiguity of our times, "I don't have a roadmap for you, but I can offer a compass."

> *Embracing uncertainty might sound like, "I don't have a roadmap for you, but I can offer a compass."*

That compass is built on principles rather than predictions, on values rather than certainties, on connections rather than control. In my conversations with leaders across industries, I hear repeatedly that the organizations thriving amid uncertainty aren't those with the most detailed five-year plans; they're those with the clearest sense of what they stand for and the most nimble capacity to adapt how they express those values as circumstances change.

When I'm working with executives navigating turbulent waters, I often invite them to consider the difference between a map and a compass. A map becomes outdated the moment the terrain changes; a compass continues to orient you regardless of how the landscape shifts. The principles that guide us—belonging, courage, grace, resilience, and purpose—are our compass points.

In Julie Cameron's words from The Artist's Way, which I've returned to repeatedly during unsettled times, "Transition creates vulnerability. The safety of the old life has been set aside. The safety of the new life is not yet in place. The passage between the two feels perilous and threatening. Our feet move unsteadily on the rope bridge slung across the jungle chasm."

This image of the rope bridge captures perfectly what so many of us are feeling—the unsteadiness beneath our feet, the awareness of the depth below. Yet Cameron continues, "And yet these feelings are illusion. I am safe and secure at all times, in all situations, however unsettling...My faith is the mountain. Events are the clouds that hide its face."

The mountain behind the clouds, which provides a grounding in what remains true regardless of what surrounds us, is what enables leadership amid uncertainty. It's what allows us to say, "I don't know exactly what's ahead, but I know who we are and what we stand for as we face it together."

As I've worked with leaders across sectors, I've noticed that those who move most effectively through uncertainty share a key quality: they've developed what psychologists call tolerance for ambiguity. I'm not talking about liking uncertainty, but about developing the capacity to function effectively within it, to make sound decisions when information is incomplete, to build meaningful connections when the ground feels unstable.

This tolerance isn't something we're born with; it's a muscle we develop through practice. Each time we face uncertainty and remain grounded in our values rather than retreating to false certainty, we strengthen that muscle. Each time we acknowledge what we don't know while affirming what we do know matters, we build that capacity.

> *Each time we acknowledge what we don't know, while affirming that what we do know matters, we build capacity.*

Cole Arthur Riley's words from Black Liturgies offer a powerful framing for this practice, "If there is any bravery to me, it is in my refusal to let fear eclipse my imagination for anything other than pain. To maintain imagination for both the beautiful and the terrible is to marry prudence and hope. This is how you fall asleep to howling."

To maintain imagination for both the beautiful and the terrible, to hold the awareness of what might go wrong alongside the vision of what might go right—this is the essence of leadership amid uncertainty. It's not about ignoring the howling winds of change; it's about developing the capacity to rest amid them, to find enough steadiness to continue the journey.

As you move through these uncertain times, I invite you to consider:

- What are the principles that remain true for you regardless of external circumstances?
- What are the values that guide you when the path forward isn't clear?
- Who are the people with whom you can join hands and walk together in the rain?

These questions don't eliminate uncertainty, but they help us navigate it with greater wisdom and humanity. They help us become the kind of leaders our VUCA/BANI world calls for—those who lead not with certainty, but with clarity of values, steady presence, and the courage to walk together through the unknown. In the end, perhaps the most potent response to uncertainty isn't the pursuit of more certainty, but the cultivation of greater capacity to move meaningfully through the unknown. It's learning to walk in the rain rather than waiting for clear skies, to hold both prudence and hope, to maintain our commitment to what matters most even when the path to achieving it isn't clearly marked.

> *In the end, perhaps the most potent response to uncertainty isn't the pursuit of more certainty, but the cultivation of greater capacity to move meaningfully through the unknown.*

# GRIEF

*recognizing what's been lost*

Grief is perhaps the most misunderstood of human experiences. We've been taught to see it as something to be managed, controlled, or worse, hidden away as if it were evidence of weakness rather than testimony to our capacity to care deeply. We measure it, trying to determine what is "appropriate," how long is "reasonable," and when we should "move on." But grief follows no timetable. It cannot be scheduled or contained within the neat boundaries our efficiency-obsessed culture might prefer.

What we're grieving now extends far beyond individual loss. We're witnessing the dissolution of systems and structures we once took for granted: healthcare, education, and even democracy itself are showing signs of strain and fracture. We're experiencing the consequences of a warming planet: catastrophic fires, floods, and storms that permanently alter landscapes and displace communities. We're navigating a media environment that leaves us simultaneously over-saturated with information and starved for wisdom.

In the workplace, this manifests in the 3:00 a.m. text message announcing your entire department has been eliminated. In the meeting invitation that turns out to be your dismissal, conducted with the efficiency of a drone strike, fifteen minutes to end a fifteen-year relationship. In watching colleagues disappear without the chance for proper goodbyes, their digital presence scrubbed as if they never existed. In realizing that the promises of loyalty and mutual respect were always conditional, subject to the whims of markets and the calculations of those who measure success only in shareholder value.

There is something profoundly disturbing about how this plays out—the swiftness, the coldness, the absence of basic human acknowledgment of what is being lost. This reflects capitalism at its most naked, stripped of the pretense that people matter beyond their immediate utility. It reveals the gap between the values organizations claim to uphold and how they behave when pressure mounts. The contradiction is jarring and disorienting. One day you're a valued team member, part of a work family, and the next you're a line item to be eliminated, a cost to be cut.

But beneath these specific manifestations lies a more fundamental grief. The grief inherent in transformation itself. Even the most welcome change involves loss. The new job means leaving colleagues who have become friends. The move to a more aligned community means saying goodbye to familiar streets and routines. The evolution into a more authentic version of yourself means releasing identities and patterns that, while limiting, provided a sense of security and belonging.

> *Even the most welcome change involves loss.*

This inherent grief is woven into the very fabric of life's cycles. The oak must release last year's leaves before new growth can emerge. The butterfly cannot take flight until the caterpillar surrenders its form. The seed must crack open and dissolve before the plant can grow. Nature shows us again and again: transformation requires letting go.

What makes our current experience particularly challenging is not just the scale and pace of change, but the way our culture relates to grief itself. We've created environments—from workplaces to social media to political discourse—where grief is treated as a private matter, something to be processed on your own time, preferably invisibly. Where mourning is compressed into the briefest of acknowledgments, if it's permitted at all. This denial of our need to grieve and mourn collectively doesn't eliminate these needs; it simply drives them underground, where they emerge in other forms: disengagement, cynicism, physical illness, damaged trust.

Grief is the internal experience of complex emotions that arise when something we value is lost or changed beyond recognition. Mourning is how we express and process that grief externally—the rituals, conversations, and practices that help us metabolize loss in community with others. Both are essential, yet both are increasingly absent from our modern landscapes.

How much grief is too much? How long should we stay with it? These questions assume that grief is something we control rather than something we experience. They reflect our cultural discomfort with emotions that don't contribute directly to productivity or positivity. But what if the measure isn't quantity or duration but quality of attention? Not how much or how long, but how wholly and honestly we're willing to be present with what is true?

I think of grief not as something we need to limit but as something we need to honor—a testament to the depth of our caring, the significance of what's been lost. The appropriate amount of time is the time it actually takes, which varies widely depending on what's been lost, the circumstances of that loss, and our individual ways of processing experience.

Some grief we move through relatively quickly; other grief becomes a companion we learn to live alongside, one that changes shape over time but never entirely disappears.

> *Grief is a testament to the depth of our caring, the significance of what's been lost.*

When loss comes without warning, without opportunity for preparation or proper closure, when it's delivered in ways that themselves feel dehumanizing, we're dealing not just with the primary loss but with a secondary trauma, the wound of how the loss occurred. This matters because how we're permitted to grieve shapes not just our healing but our collective capacity to create more humane systems.

What would it look like to create spaces, both within organizations and within our broader communities, where grief and mourning are recognized as essential aspects of our shared humanity? Where endings of all kinds are treated with the same care and attention as beginnings? Where we acknowledge that significant changes represent real losses that deserve to be honored rather than minimized or denied?

In our workplaces, it might look like creating time for proper goodbyes when teams are disbanded. Like acknowledging contributions publicly and specifically before people depart. Like rituals that mark transitions with dignity rather than treating them as failures to be hidden. Like leaders who dare to be present with the pain their decisions cause, rather than distancing themselves through clinical language or delegating the human conversations to others.

In our communities, it might look like creating meaningful ways to acknowledge collective losses—the closing of

# GRIEF

a beloved local business, the decline of a field of expertise, the redevelopment of a neighborhood, the effects of environmental damage on places we've cherished. It might include the quiet erosion of entire movements, like the retreat from DEI efforts in workplaces, where years of emotional labor, hope, and hard-won progress have too often been dismantled without reflection or ritual. It might involve reclaiming ancestral mourning practices that helped people metabolize loss together rather than in isolation. It might mean creating new rituals that honor contemporary experiences of grief for which we have no established ceremonies.

In our societal discourse, it might involve making space for the grief that undergirds so many of our political divisions—grief for changing ways of life, for lost certainties, for shifting power dynamics. What if we recognized that beneath the anger and polarization often lies unacknowledged loss? Loss that, when addressed directly, could open pathways to more productive dialogue.

There's wisdom in considering a different kind of "too much" when it comes to grief—not too much feeling, but too much isolation. Grief becomes most dangerous when we face it alone, when we're cut off from the witnessing presence of others who can help us carry what feels unbearable. This is where mourning becomes essential, not as a timetable for "getting over it," but as a shared practice that helps us integrate loss into our ongoing life rather than being defined by it.

> *Grief becomes most dangerous when we face it alone, when we're cut off from the witnessing presence of others who can help us carry what feels unbearable.*

Mourning rituals have existed in every culture throughout human history precisely because they answer this deep need for collective acknowledgment of loss. They provide structure when everything feels chaotic, community when we feel most alone, and meaning when events seem senseless. Yet in our modern contexts, we've largely abandoned these practices, leaving people to navigate significant transitions without the support such rituals provide.

What if we reclaimed some of this wisdom? What if we created contemporary mourning practices that help us honor the full spectrum of losses we're experiencing—from the personal to the professional to the planetary? Not to wallow in them indefinitely, but to move through them with integrity rather than around them through denial. To acknowledge what's true, that genuine relationships have ended, that meaningful work has been disrupted, that communities carefully built over time have been dismantled, that landscapes we've loved have been altered beyond recognition, without implying that these losses define the entirety of what's possible next.

Because this is the ultimate purpose of grief and mourning—not to keep us fixated on what's been lost, but to help us integrate that loss into a new story that honors what was while remaining open to what might be. To find what psychologist Francis Weller calls "the grace in the wound"—the way loss, when fully acknowledged, can deepen our capacity for presence, connection, and meaning.

This integration doesn't happen on a prescribed timeline. It unfolds according to its own rhythm, influenced by the depth of the loss, the circumstances surrounding it, the resources available to us, and countless other factors unique to each situation and person. The question isn't "How long should we grieve?" but "Are we giving this loss the attention it deserves?" Not to magnify it beyond proportion, but to acknowledge its real impact on our lives, our communities, our sense of what's possible.

When we try to skip this phase, rushing from loss directly to new opportunity without pausing to honor what's been disrupted, we carry the unprocessed grief with us, where it colors everything that follows. We might find ourselves unable to fully engage with what's emerging, held back by the gravitational pull of what remains unacknowledged. Or we might throw ourselves into new beginnings with frenetic energy, using activity and achievement to outrun the feelings we're afraid to face.

In these times of profound change and uncertainty, when so many of our familiar landscapes are shifting beyond recognition, grief becomes not an obstacle to transformation but its very doorway. It asks us to stop our habitual movement long enough to feel the full weight of what's changing. To acknowledge what we've invested, what we've built, what we've valued, and how painful it is to see these things altered or dismantled.

> *Grief asks us to stop our habitual movement long enough to feel the full weight of what's changing.*

This pause isn't a detour from the journey of becoming; it's an essential part of that journey. It's how we honor the reality that transformative change involves real loss alongside real possibility. It's how we maintain our humanity in systems that often seem designed to strip it away. It's how we resist the pressure to treat ourselves and others as merely functional units rather than whole, feeling beings with complex inner lives that deserve respect.

May we find the courage to create such spaces, for ourselves and each other. May we resist the cultural pressure to move through loss at the pace of quarterly reports rather than at the pace of the human heart. May we remember that our capacity to grieve fully is inseparable from our capacity to love deeply, and that both are essential aspects of what makes us most fully human. And may we remember, too, that grief is not meant to be carried alone. In the presence of others, witnessed and shared, it becomes not only more bearable but more transformative.

*May we resist the cultural pressure to move through loss at the pace of quarterly reports rather than at the pace of the human heart.*

# STILLNESS

## *the wisdom of pause*

In the midst of winter, I often find myself standing at the edge of my home in the Catskill Mountains, watching moonlight stretch long shadows across the snow. The trees, bare and unmoving, aren't dead. They're simply practicing a different kind of living: quiet, inward, nearly invisible to anyone not paying close attention. The silence is thick, brimming with presence and with something that feels, oddly, like possibility.

This stillness speaks in a slow rhythm, almost like breath, just beneath awareness. It tells me a story of patience, of quiet labor that begins when the visible part of us goes still. Work that resists recognition. And it reminds me—gently, but insistently—that change doesn't stop when we stop hustling, producing, moving. It only moves deeper underground.

Clark Strand, a local author who wrote *Waking Up to the Dark*, walks these same Catskill forests at night. He calls it "unplugging from the billion-watt culture" to touch "an ancient reservoir of ancestral wisdom and inspiration." At first, I wasn't sure what he meant. Now, I think I do. Stillness, I've come to believe, isn't the absence of motion. It's a different kind of presence—one that lets us hear what constant noise drowns out.

The trees around me seem to understand this better than I do. Nature moves in its own time, through ebb and flow, through sowing and reaping—and yes, resting. The quiet now? It's just a pause. A long, slow in-breath. Not an ending. Not even stillness, exactly. More like a gathering.

What if we could live this way, too? Not seeing stillness as stagnation, but as preparation. Not a lack, but a beginning we don't yet recognize.

In our always-on, hyper-connected world, we've lost the natural rhythm between stillness and movement, the pulse that once shaped our days, our seasons, our bodies. Night used to bring darkness, and with it, rest. Reflection. Now we light it up and keep going. The seasons once demanded pause, a letting go. Now, with climate control and next-day shipping, we live in the illusion of perpetual summer. As if harvest can come without fallow.

The antidote to an incomprehensible world isn't more motion, more striving, more signalling. Sometimes, strange as it sounds, it's stillness.

> **The antidote to an incomprehensible world isn't more motion, more striving, more signalling. Sometimes, strange as it sounds, it's stillness.**

I'm learning this slowly. And unevenly. I spent years in New York City, riding the momentum like it was virtue. You can rush through entire seasons there without noticing. I did. Head down, moving fast, mistaking motion for meaning.

But here, in the quiet of the mountains, I've begun to discover something else. A different kind of productivity. One that values the dark, the dormant, the pause before the leap. The moment of listening before the answer arrives.

It's strange, even now, to write this. I've always believed that activism meant action, movement, visibility, and effort. But I'm beginning to understand that real change doesn't come only from doing. It also comes from waiting. From creating the conditions inside ourselves for wisdom to surface.

In stillness, we start to notice again. The faint signals. The shift in weather, in mood, in pattern. The subtle signs that something's no longer working. That something else might be possible. In stillness, we hear the voice beneath the noise—quiet, but clear. Sometimes, it's been speaking all along.

Stillness doesn't make us passive. It makes us permeable. We absorb more. Sense more. Reflect instead of react. We bend where before we might have broken.

> *Stillness doesn't make us passive.*
> *It makes us permeable.*

Just as winter isn't the end of the growing season, stillness isn't the end of leadership. It's where it begins. The kind of leadership that doesn't rush to speak, but waits to resonate. That doesn't cling to knowing, but learns to understand. That doesn't just do but chooses to *be*.

When I work with leaders, I see what happens in the absence of stillness. The panicked decisions. The strategies that shatter under pressure. The improvisation that never comes, because there's no space for intuition to enter. I see people leading without ever listening. Solving problems that haven't been named. Progressing without direction.

But sometimes, if we're willing to pause just long enough to really stop, we discover something different. We realize the answers weren't missing. Just buried. Waiting. Asking us to quiet down enough to notice them.

This kind of stillness isn't resignation. It's attention. It's presence. And it's powerful.

Standing in the moonlight of the Catskills, my breath curling into the cold, I feel it again, that sense of connection. Not to certainty, but to something more profound. Beyond the immediate. Beyond the urgent. Beyond even what I can name.

This is the gift stillness offers. Not escape, but a way back into relationship. Not clarity through control, but clarity through presence. Not answers, but a deeper way of holding the questions.

The trees know this. The seasons know this. Even our bodies know this, if we're willing to listen.

# SURRENDER

*Letting go of what no longer serves*

There's a moment in metamorphosis that scientists call histolysis, when a caterpillar's body completely dissolves inside its chrysalis. The creature becomes what they call "bug soup"—a nutrient-rich slurry that will eventually fuel its reconstruction into a butterfly. There's no bouncing back from bug soup. And maybe that's precisely the point.

Transformation, especially the kind that demands surrender, is often framed as a personal virtue—resilience, adaptability, strength. But what does it actually require of us? I've been asking that question through the lens of my own story. For twenty years, I ran a company with my name on the door. We generated millions in revenue, shaped how organizations approached diversity, equity, and inclusion, and wrote books that changed conversations. And from the outside, it probably looked like a perfect example of resilience, adaptability, growth, and impact.

But underneath that success story, I was carrying what I've come to call the "nuclear waste" of leadership, those experiences of betrayal, loss, and misalignment that we're told to push past in the name of being resilient. We bury this waste deep, hoping it won't leak. But what if that burial is exactly what's keeping us from real transformation?

Scientists tell us that when a caterpillar enters its chrysalis, its immune system attacks its own body. The old self must be seen as foreign for the new self to emerge. This isn't just poetic or cruel; it's literally how nature handles profound change.

I see this playing out right now in the DEI field, a field I helped build. We're watching something similar to that chrysalis moment. The old frameworks, the familiar arguments, the ways we've always done this work—they're dissolving. And our collective immune response? We're fighting it. We're rebranding initiatives. We're doubling down on old metrics, trying to hold companies accountable using the same tools that haven't fully worked before.

But what if, like that caterpillar, we need to let our immune systems dismantle what no longer serves? What if this moment of apparent destruction is the precursor to something new?

> *What if this moment of apparent destruction is the precursor to something new?*

The maple tree's annual journey shows us this wisdom: the vibrant surge of spring sap rising, the full canopy of summer leaves converting sunlight to energy, the slowing of autumn when the work is done, and finally the necessary letting go of leaves. The tree doesn't cling to its leaves out of fear or ego. It doesn't try to maintain summer's peak forever.

Or consider tide pools on a rocky coast: the rush of new water bringing nutrients, the rich ecosystem thriving at high tide, the gradual receding revealing what's been accomplished, and the courage to empty completely. Each cycle creates the conditions for the next.

Even the soil itself teaches us this pattern: the burst of spring growth, the abundant harvest, the field lying fallow, and the decomposition of what's finished. Without that final phase of breaking down, there can be no renewal. The fallow time isn't empty; it's essential, a sacred pause where the unseen work of restoration happens beneath the surface, preparing for the next cycle of abundance.

Nature shows us how to yield to necessary endings. But in our systems—in business, in leadership, in social change—we behave as though we're exempt from these laws. As if endless output and constant momentum will save us. As if we can skip the surrender. We're like trees trying to keep their leaves year round, tide pools refusing to empty, fields never allowed to rest. We maintain facades and bury our nuclear waste, hoping it doesn't leak.

But surrender isn't collapse; it's conscious release in service of regeneration.

> *Surrender isn't collapse.*
> *It's conscious release in*
> *service of regeneration.*

When I sold my company last year, people kept congratulating me. Someone even sent flowers with a note saying, "Here are your flowers. Thank you for building what you've built." But what they couldn't see was the depth of the grief I was experiencing, not just for my company, but for the field and the work itself. The stories we'd told about what progress looked like no longer held.

We are now watching entire systems become uninhabitable, not just organizations, but whole ways of thinking about change and progress. The old metrics, the familiar frameworks, the comfortable narratives—they're all turning into bug soup.

The caterpillar spends nearly a third of its life dissolving—becoming unrecognizable—before something new can take shape. And yet we expect leaders, systems, and selves to transform overnight, without pause, without mess. Maybe the art of falling apart isn't about failing or breaking down. Perhaps it's about having the courage to let go of who we've been so we can become what's needed next.

> *We expect leaders, systems, and selves to transform overnight, without pause, without mess.*

Transmutation isn't about maintaining the status quo while adding a few new features. It's about allowing a complete dissolution, breaking down to elemental components, so that something wholly new can emerge, informed by but not identical to what came before.

In a world where nothing feels certain and everything feels brittle, this willingness to break down completely may be our most radical act. Not as a surrender to destruction, but as a surrender to the natural process of rebirth that has always governed life on this planet.

When we resist the unraveling by clinging to roles, identities, or beliefs that once served us, we don't just stall progress. We starve the future of what could emerge from our release. We mistake survival for thriving, maintenance for growth.

The question before us isn't whether we can keep what we've built intact through the storms of change. The question is whether we have the courage to let it dissolve when its time has come, trusting that what emerges from that dissolution will be precisely what's needed next.

I invite you to consider: What part of you, your work, your field is asking to dissolve, not in defeat, but in trust? What might be waiting on the other side of surrender?

# PART 2
# Returning To What's True

# TRUTH

*returning to what matters*

There's a kind of knowing that doesn't come through thinking. It doesn't arrive through headlines or hashtags or expert takes; it hums beneath all that. You don't chase it. You notice it. A low frequency that registers in the body before the mind can catch up. Not the kind of clarity that's handed down by authority, but the kind that rises uninvited from somewhere deeper.

We find ourselves navigating what many have called a "post-truth" era. A time when shared reality itself seems to have fractured, when competing versions of events claim equal validity, when traditional sources of authority have lost their power to create consensus. The maps we once relied upon to orient ourselves collectively have disintegrated, leaving each of us to make sense of a territory that seems to shift beneath our feet.

This disorientation is not accidental. It serves particular interests to keep us confused, reactive, and disconnected from our own discernment. When we lose trust in our capacity to recognize what's real, we become more susceptible to manipulation, more likely to outsource our thinking—whether to those who speak with superficial certainty or to algorithms that claim to know us better than we know ourselves—and more vulnerable to the appeal of simple answers in a complex world.

Yet, within this very challenge lies an invitation. If we can no longer rely on consensus reality to orient us, perhaps we are being called to develop a different relationship with truth altogether, one less dependent on external validation and more grounded in internal coherence. Not truth as something handed down from authorities we trust, but truth as something we actively engage with, test against our lived experience, and refine through relationship with others who are similarly committed to what's real.

This isn't relativism (the notion that all perspectives are equally valid, that truth is merely a matter of opinion). It's precisely the opposite. It's the recognition that in a landscape flooded with misinformation, partial truths, and deliberate distortions, discerning what's real requires more from us, not less. It demands a quality of attention, a commitment to looking beneath surface appearances, a willingness to hold complexity rather than retreating to the comfort of simplistic certainties.

I think of the forge, where metal is heated until malleable, then shaped through the skilled application of pressure. Our relationship with truth undergoes a similar process. Life experiences heat us to the point where rigid certainties can no longer hold. Encounters with perspectives different from ours apply pressure that reshapes what we thought we knew. If we resist this process, clinging to brittle forms of knowing, we become fragile, prone to shattering when reality challenges our beliefs. But if we can surrender to it—not abandoning discernment, but allowing our understanding to be refined through contact with what's real—we develop a different kind of strength, one that bends without breaking, that can incorporate new information without losing its essential integrity.

> *Like metal melting in a forge, life experiences heat us to the point where rigid certainties can no longer hold.*

This forging doesn't happen in isolation. Truth emerges not just from individual introspection but from the friction of genuine dialogue, from allowing our perspectives to be challenged and expanded through relationship with others. Not just any others but those who share our commitment to what's real rather than what's comfortable or convenient. Those willing to say, "I might be wrong," and mean it. Those capable of holding the tension between conviction and humility.

This approach to truth invites us to become archaeologists of our own knowing—to excavate beneath the surface of received wisdom and examine what we find there. Which beliefs do we hold simply because they were handed to us by family, education, or culture? Which serve interests other than our own? Which have we adopted out of fear rather than clear seeing? And conversely, which arise from our direct experience of life? Which have been tested and refined through honest dialogue? Which align with our deepest values and sense of purpose?

This excavation isn't about rejecting everything we've been taught. It's about developing a more conscious relationship with it—keeping what withstands scrutiny, releasing what doesn't, remaining open to new understanding without abandoning discernment. It's about recognizing that truth is neither purely subjective (merely what I happen to believe) nor purely objective (existing entirely independent of the knower), but emerges in the dynamic relationship between perception and reality, between individual experience and collective wisdom.

> *Truth emerges in the dynamic relationship between perception and reality, between individual experience and collective wisdom.*

In a world where external agreement can no longer be assumed, we might consider a different metaphor for truth, not as a fixed point on a map that everyone must acknowledge, but as an internal compass that orients us even when the landmarks have disappeared. This compass doesn't point to what's popular or politically expedient or personally comfortable. It points to what feels authentic when we consult our deepest knowing, what remains consistent across contexts, what aligns our words with our actions, and our actions with our values.

Developing this internal compass requires practice. It means cultivating the capacity to distinguish between the immediate reactivity of our conditioned responses and the deeper knowing that emerges when we create space to listen beneath the noise. It means learning to recognize the sensation of alignment, to how truth feels in our bodies, not just how it registers in our minds. It means noticing when we're speaking or acting from integrity versus when we're being moved by fear, external pressure, or unconscious patterns.

This isn't easy work. Our internal sensors have been calibrated by the very culture we're trying to see beyond. Our perception is shaped by biases we may not recognize. Our capacity for self-deception is profound. This is why truth-seeking is ultimately a relational practice, one that requires both solitary reflection and engagement with others who can help us see our blind spots, who can offer perspectives beyond our limited vantage point, and who can hold us accountable to our own stated values and commitments.

In organizations, when leaders claim to value truth but punish those who speak it, they create cultures of strategic silence where real issues go unaddressed until they become crises. When they prioritize comfort over clarity, they make decisions based on what people want to hear rather than what they need to know. When they confuse loyalty with agreement, they surround themselves with voices that echo rather than challenge their thinking.

The alternative isn't brutal honesty that disregards impact, but what we might call "caring truth," communication that honors both reality and relationship, that seeks to be both accurate and attuned to how messages are received. This kind of truth-telling requires tremendous discernment. It asks us to consider not just what is true, but which truths need expression in a given moment, in what way, for what purpose. It invites us to speak from clarity rather than reaction, from care rather than righteousness.

Ultimately, the work of truth in these disorienting times isn't about finding certainty to cling to or authorities to trust without question. It's about developing our capacity to navigate complexity with integrity, to remain oriented toward what matters most even when external signals are confusing or contradictory. It's about reclaiming our agency as discerners of what's real rather than passive consumers of others' certainties.

This approach to truth won't provide the comfort of certainty in uncertain times. It won't tell us exactly what to believe or whom to trust without question. It will leave us with more nuanced questions rather than simple answers. But it offers something more valuable—a way of relating to reality that neither denies complexity nor surrenders to confusion, that remains oriented toward what's real even when consensus about reality has fractured.

In practical terms, this means approaching truth not as a possession to defend but as a direction to orient toward. It means holding our current understanding with what Zen practitioners call "beginner's mind," neither clinging to what we think we know nor abandoning our capacity for discernment, but remaining genuinely open to refinement through encounters with perspectives different from our own. It means developing the capacity to hold paradoxes, to live with questions that don't resolve neatly into answers, to embrace the both/and nature of complex realities rather than reducing them to either/or propositions.

In times of distortion and noise, the most revolutionary act may be this quiet insistence on staying aligned with what rings true in our bodies, our relationships, our lived experience. Not as a retreat from collective reality, but as a commitment to engaging it more consciously. Not as a rejection of facts, but as a recognition that facts alone don't create meaning; we make sense of them through frameworks of value and purpose that we must continually refine.

> *In times of distortion and noise, the most revolutionary act may be this quiet insistence on staying aligned with what rings true in our bodies, our relationships, our lived experience.*

May we find the courage for this work of discernment. May we create spaces where truth can be sought together rather than weaponized against one another. And may we remember that in a world of manufactured certainties, the most trustworthy compass remains this internal alignment, this resonance between what we perceive, what we believe, what we say, and how we live.

# WISDOM

*drawing on deeper knowing*

We are living in the most information-saturated era in human history. The average person today is exposed to more data in a single day than previous generations encountered in a lifetime. Google promises to "organize the world's information," and in many ways, it has. Answers are always just a search—or now, a prompt—away.

But for all our access to knowledge, wisdom remains stubbornly rare.

Knowledge can be accumulated, collected, and downloaded. We gather facts, we study, we learn methodologies and frameworks. But wisdom sits deeper in our bones. It's what emerges when knowledge is metabolized, integrated, and transformed by suffering, by joy, by the fullness of our human experience.

You can see this difference clearly in the rise of artificial intelligence. AI has absorbed the collective knowledge of the internet, more data than any one human could possibly hold. And yet, it routinely misses the nuance, the depth, the discernment that defines true wisdom. Because wisdom isn't just about knowing more; it's about knowing how to be in the world, how to respond with care, with humility, with grace. That can't be downloaded. It has to be lived.

> *Wisdom isn't just about knowing more; it's about knowing how to be in the world, how to respond with care, with humility, with grace.*

We each carry unique wisdom born from our particular journey through life. The parts of ourselves we've had to hide, the battles we've fought, the privileges we've had or lacked—all of these shape the particular resonance of our instrument, the wisdom accessible only through our specific life experience.

That lived experience becomes the lens through which we pull wisdom from knowledge.

Some of that wisdom arrives suddenly, through moments of rupture or revelation. I think back to when I realized I was queer, in my early twenties. Coming out wasn't just about acknowledging my sexual orientation; it was a profound awakening to see the structures of the world differently. Suddenly, I could perceive systems of power and privilege that had been invisible to me before. I began to question everything I'd been taught about how the world worked, who belonged where, and what success looked like. That awakening was its own form of wisdom—a deeper knowing that what I'd accepted as "just the way things are" was actually a constructed reality that could be questioned, challenged, and reimagined.

When you've had to forge your own path because the traditional one wasn't available to you, you develop a different relationship to authority, to convention, to "how things have always been done." You learn to trust your inner guidance because external navigation systems weren't built for your journey.

This is the kind of wisdom that lives in the margins, in the experiences of those who've had to create their own maps. When conventional systems fail us, when the maps no longer match the territory, we need access to ways of knowing that aren't bound by the same assumptions that created our current crises.

The wisdom that emerges in those moments isn't always linear or prescriptive. It doesn't offer tidy solutions or guaranteed outcomes. Instead, it offers something subtler and more enduring: a compass rather than a map. A felt sense of direction rather than step-by-step instructions. This kind of wisdom helps us navigate uncertainty with grace, hold complexity without collapsing it, and meet challenge with creativity rather than reactivity.

Much of what we consider wisdom in dominant culture is quite limited, privileging certain kinds of knowing (rational, analytical, credential-based) while dismissing others (intuitive, embodied, ancestral). A hallmark of patriarchal systems has been the systematic devaluation of wisdom traditions associated with women, with indigenous cultures, with any group that threatens the established power structure.

Consider the wisdom embedded in indigenous approaches to land stewardship: understanding ecosystems as complex webs of relationship rather than resources to be extracted. Or the wisdom of women who, across cultures, have often been the keepers of community knowledge, the ones who know how to sustain life when systems collapse.

These forms of wisdom haven't been valued in our efficiency-obsessed, productivity-driven culture. But they contain precisely the kind of knowing we need to navigate our complex, interconnected challenges.

Our educational systems and professional cultures have trained us to chase certainty, to have answers, to project confidence even when we're confused. But what if the wisest path is in developing the capacity to say, "I don't know yet, let's explore this together?"

> *What if the wisest path is in developing the capacity to say, "I don't know yet, let's explore this together?"*

Wade Davis, a former NFL player turned educator and inclusion strategist, speaks powerfully about what he calls being "disinterested in being right" and even being willing to let go of being seen as a good person. It's a radical act of humility in a culture that rewards performance and perfection. But when we release the need to posture, we open ourselves, and others, to real learning.

True wisdom often reveals itself not in what we proclaim to know, but in the questions we're willing to sit with, in the curiosity we bring to complexity rather than the impulse to simplify it away. One of my favorite questions to sit with personally is "What do I not yet know?" And when we find ourselves in moments of dissolution, when what we thought we knew no longer serves, we may be in the midst of wisdom's most profound work.

The chaos is not failure; it's transformation in process. When we learn to see these moments as the invisible hand of wisdom at work—the universe's method in the madness, so to speak—we might just find comfort, or even clarity, in the unknown.

How do we access this deeper knowing? How do we mine our experiences for the wisdom they contain?

First, we need to slow down. Wisdom doesn't emerge at the speed of efficiency. It reveals itself in reflection, in contemplation, in the spaciousness we create to hear the quieter voices within ourselves and our communities.

Second, we must be willing to listen to the wisdom of our bodies. So much of what we "know" lives not in our logical minds but in our physical experience—in the resonance we feel when something rings true, in the contraction we sense when something violates our values. Our bodies often know before our minds can articulate.

Third, we need to honor the wisdom that comes from failure, from getting it wrong, from the humbling experiences that break open our certainty and make space for new understanding. Some of the most profound wisdom I carry comes from moments where my assumptions were shattered, where I had to rebuild my understanding from the ground up.

Finally, we must recognize that wisdom is collective as well as individual. Wisdom lies in understanding that we are simultaneously insignificant on a cosmic scale and profoundly significant in the relationships and communities we touch. The deepest kind of knowing emerges not in isolation but in relationship, in the interplay of diverse perspectives, in the wisdom that can only be accessed when we come together across divides.

Ultimately, wisdom isn't something we possess but something we practice, returning to the forge, again and again. It's not a destination we reach but a way of moving through the world. It's being willing to sit with complexity rather than rushing to simplicity. It's trusting process when outcomes are unclear. It's remembering what matters most when everything feels uncertain.

## Wisdom

*Wisdom isn't something we
possess but something we practice.*

In these challenging times, wisdom calls us to show up fully for what is, while remaining open to what might be. It invites us to draw on deeper knowing not as escape from the often unpleasant realities of our world, but as a way to move through it with more grace, more courage, and more truth.

# COURAGE

*presence in the face of fear*

I used to imagine courage as running into a burning house while everyone else slept inside, unaware of the flames. I was the one charging in—trying to wake them, trying to warn them, trying to help. But over time, that image began to trouble me. Why was I always the one running back into the fire? Especially when some didn't want to be awakened at all?

These questions unraveled something important. Courage isn't just about boldness. It's not always noble or clean. Sometimes, it's just choosing to step toward the heat when your whole body aches to walk away.

> *Courage isn't just about boldness. It's not always noble or clean. Sometimes, it's just choosing to step toward the heat when your whole body aches to walk away.*

We tend to think of courage as fearlessness. But the root of the word—*cor*, from Latin—means "heart." At its center, courage is about heart-fullness. It's about bringing your whole, trembling, breakable heart to situations that scare you, stretch you, maybe even undo you.

I've seen this kind of courage show up in quiet, uncelebrated ways. In people who choose to lower their waterline and reveal more of themselves than they feels safe with. The LGBTQ+ employee who comes out at work, not knowing how their team will respond. The ally who interrupts a microaggression, even when their voice shakes. The leader who says, "I don't know," when it would be easier to fake certainty.

This is the courage we're most in need of now. Not the grand, cinematic kind. But the daily, often invisible kind. The courage to be real when it's far easier to perform. To stay present when everything in you wants to disappear.

In my work, I've learned that this kind of courage isn't something we're born with. It's something we build. Like a callus or a skill. Joze Piranian, a lifelong stutterer turned international speaker, calls it "millions of micro moments of bravery." Moments where you do the thing that scares you, not once, but again and again, until something shifts.

And that's the heart of it: not the absence of fear, but a different relationship to it. Courageous people aren't fearless. They've just stopped waiting for fear to leave before they act.

> *Courageous people aren't fearless. They've just stopped waiting for fear to leave before they act.*

Someone once told me, "The bad news about fear is that it never goes away. And the good news about fear is that it never goes away." I didn't fully understand that at first. But over time, I've come to see the truth in it.

When we stop treating fear as something to eliminate, we can begin to move with it. Not around it. Not after it passes. With it. Through it. We stop waiting for permission from comfort, and instead learn to act in its company.

Here's what doesn't get said enough: courage rarely feels good while it's happening. When I lost my singing voice, the one I'd built a career around, it didn't feel like a brave pivot. It felt like collapse. When I've challenged people in power, it hasn't felt like moral clarity. It's felt like my stomach twisting in knots. And when I "come out" on stage, again and again, to audiences of potentially hostile strangers, it doesn't feel empowering. It feels exposing. Like I'm standing there with no armor, unsure whether I'll be met with understanding or resistance.

Courage is often messy. It's stumbling through a difficult conversation. It's shaking while you speak. It's the vulnerability of saying something true without knowing how it will land. Nothing about it is polished. It's raw. It's human. And that's why it matters.

That's why real, sustainable courage requires compassion, not just for others, but for ourselves. If we're going to keep stepping into discomfort, we have to learn how to hold ourselves gently while we do. To recognize that courage doesn't mean we always get it right. It means we keep showing up, even when we falter. Especially then.

> *If we're going to keep stepping into discomfort, we have to learn how to hold ourselves gently while we do.*

It's not a fixed trait. It's a muscle. And like any muscle, it grows through use—sometimes stronger because of failure, not despite it. Every time we move toward something that matters, even while afraid, we stretch that capacity just a little more.

There's another layer to this, one that gets overlooked: the courage to change. To say, "I used to believe this. I see it differently now." Or, "I made a mistake. I'm learning." In a world obsessed with certainty, there's something radical about that kind of humility. Something deeply brave.

And then there's the quiet courage we extend to others. The kind that says: I see you trying. I see you growing. I'll stand beside you, even when your process is imperfect. That's the kind of courage that holds space, not just for resistance to harm, but for someone else's transformation.

On the podcast, we often talk about calling in instead of calling out. It's not about letting harm slide. It's about believing that people can change, and being willing to stay in the room while they do. That, too, is courage. Not just standing up against something, but standing with someone who is trying to become more whole.

And let's be honest: most of us didn't get where we are without someone doing that for us. Someone who dared to offer truth, even when it was hard. Someone who risked being dismissed or misunderstood so that we might grow. None of us got here alone.

And that's the thing about courage: it's rarely sustainable in isolation. This is a quieter kind of bravery, of intellectual and emotional courage—the willingness to stay open when it would be easier to shut down. To stay curious instead of certain. In a world addicted to polarization and performance, this kind of openness might be our best chance at healing. It's what allows authentic dialogue to happen. It's what keeps the door from slamming shut—on others, and on ourselves.

I often return to a question someone once asked me, "How do we create change when the stakes are high, the road is blocked, and we are exhausted?"

I don't think there's a single answer. But I know this: we don't do it alone. Courage becomes possible and sustainable when practiced in community.

> *Courage becomes possible and sustainable when practiced in community.*

Because none of us can be brave every day. There are mornings when the fire is too hot, the air too thick, the people too unwilling to wake. On those days, we need someone else to go in first. Someone to carry the torch while we catch our breath.

That's what community offers. We take turns being strong. We remind each other why we keep showing up. We hold space for fear, and we don't shame the pause. We say, "Rest. I've got you for now."

And in that exchange, something remarkable happens. Courage grows, not just individually, but collectively. It becomes a shared resource. A practice that moves between us.

The most courageous people I know still feel fear. But they've stopped letting it drive. They've found something that matters more than comfort: whether it's justice, truth, belonging, or love. Something that calls them forward even when their knees shake.

This, I believe, is how we build courage in an overwhelming world. Not through bravado. Not through certainty. But through presence. Through practice. Through staying in the room.

It's not the loudest courage we need right now, but the truest. The courage to remain open-hearted when cynicism tempts us to close. The courage to speak when silence feels safer. The courage to hope, even when we've been disappointed before.

And maybe most of all, the courage to keep stepping into that burning building—not because we're sure we'll succeed, but because something in us knows that transformation is still possible, and people are worth the risk.

Because in the end, courage isn't measured by outcome. It's measured by presence. By how fully we show up, heart in hand, for the work that matters most.

# RESILIENCE

*developing strength through difficulty*

There's an image that often comes to mind when I think about resilience. It's the image of bamboo bending impossibly low to the ground during a fierce storm. While mighty oaks crack and fall around it, the bamboo survives by yielding, by finding strength in flexibility rather than rigidity. When the storm passes, it slowly rises again, perhaps changed by the experience but fundamentally whole.

The metaphor of strength through flexibility has walked with me throughout my journey, a truth I've returned to time and again as I've navigated the unpredictable terrain of personal and professional change. But resilience isn't just about weathering storms; it's about what happens within us as we bend.

It's also about how we rise. How we recover. How we metabolize what the storm has taught us—integrating pain, insight, disruption, and grace. Resilience isn't just the will to change, but the willingness to be changed. To let experience shape us without hardening us. To emerge not untouched, but more whole.

*Resilience isn't just the will to change, but the willingness to be changed.*

For many of us, resilience feels like a destination. Our conventional wisdom often speaks of "failing forward," suggesting a linear progression toward some idealized, more perfect state. Yet I've come to understand that resilience isn't about forward momentum at all; it's about inhabiting that liminal space where we exist in constant testing, redefinition, and nonlinear becoming. It's not about progressing toward an endpoint but dancing with uncertainty in an ongoing process of dissolution and reformation, where each challenge invites us to reimagine what strength might mean in this particular moment.

When we encounter significant challenges or setbacks, something curious happens. We often experience what feels like breaking: our assumptions shatter, our plans collapse, and our understanding of ourselves comes into question. This breaking open can feel devastating in the moment, a disintegration of everything we believed to be solid. Yet within this breaking lies a profound opportunity. Just as pressure transforms coal into diamonds, difficulty can catalyze growth that might otherwise never occur.

The Japanese art of kintsugi repairs broken pottery with gold, creating something more beautiful and valuable than the original intact piece. Our breaks, too, can become the very places where not just our greatest strength emerges, but where unexpected beauty blossoms, where the golden seams of our healing transform what was broken into something more luminous than before.

But there's wisdom in not rushing the repair. In staying with the cracks a while. Letting the fracture teach us before we try to seal it. Real resilience isn't about snapping back or fixing quickly; it's about honoring the depth of what was lost and allowing the process of mending to take the time it needs. Healing is not a performance; it's a presence. And sometimes, the most courageous thing we can do is simply remain in the in-between: unfinished, tender, and still becoming.

The idea that our wounds can become wellsprings of wisdom isn't just poetic; it's a fundamental truth about human development. The question becomes not whether we will face difficulty, but how we will allow it to shape us. Will we resist the breaking, fighting to maintain an illusion of control? Or will we surrender to the process, trusting that we contain within ourselves the capacity to be remade? Like the caterpillar in its chrysalis, we too must sometimes fully dissolve before we can emerge as something entirely new—not merely a stronger version of our former selves, but a fundamentally transformed being.

To truly develop resilience, we must first acknowledge our vulnerability. The more we can sit with our fragility, recognizing the places where we feel tender or uncertain, the more genuine our resilience becomes. This runs counter to our cultural narratives about "bouncing back" or "pushing through." True resilience isn't about denying difficulty or pretending we're unaffected. It's about creating space for our full experience—the grief, the fear, the doubt—while simultaneously holding the possibility of our own renewal.

I'm reminded of what I've learned through the LGBTQ+ community's history of resilience. For decades, queer people have faced systemic barriers, discrimination, and sometimes violence. Yet from this difficulty has emerged not just survival, but profound innovation, culture-making, and joy. This isn't resilience as mere endurance, but as creative transformation, turning what could destroy into what ultimately liberates. When I reflect on my journey of coming out, losing my singing voice to injury, pivoting my career multiple times, and building a business during economic uncertainty, I recognize that each difficult passage contained its own particular wisdom. The resilience I developed wasn't a generic "toughness" but a specific response to specific challenges. And woven through this form of resilience is the quiet acknowledgment that future challenges will continue to roll toward me like waves in the ocean—inevitable. Inexorable. Not as interruptions to some idealized steady state, but as the very rhythm of a fully lived life.

> *From difficulty emerges not just survival, but profound innovation, culture-making, and joy.*

While resilience is deeply personal, it doesn't exist in isolation. Our ability to remain flexible in the face of challenge is profoundly influenced by the systems and communities surrounding us. This understanding shifts the conversation from *Why aren't you more resilient?* to *What conditions support human resilience?*

In truth, very few organizations truly normalize both strength and struggle. More often, resilience is framed through the lens of individual grit, while success is celebrated and the messiness of the journey is quietly bypassed. The vulnerability it takes to name fatigue, to admit uncertainty, or to share the emotional toll of change is rarely met with structured support, let alone cultural permission.

And yet, I've witnessed glimpses of what's possible. When teams develop shared language for navigating difficulty, when leaders model emotional honesty without sacrificing vision, resilience becomes more than a personal trait; it becomes a communal practice. In these rare but powerful environments, resilience isn't demanded; it's cultivated.

The most grounded leaders I know understand this intuitively. They recognize that their capacity to bend without breaking is directly connected to how they create space for others to do the same. They know that expecting resilience without providing support is like asking for a harvest without planting seeds or providing water.

Perhaps the least understood aspect of resilience is what happens in the spaces between challenges—the quiet work of renewal that prepares us for the next storm. This isn't about "self-care" in its commercialized form, but about the deeper practices that restore our sense of possibility and connection. Renewal might look like time in nature, creative expression, spiritual practice, or meaningful connection with others. It's about replenishing what difficulty depletes, about remembering who we are beyond our struggles. Without this rhythm of renewal, resilience becomes depleted; we end up running on empty, mistaking exhaustion for strength. I think about the countless leaders who've shared with me their practices of reflection and restoration—the CEO who writes poetry before dawn, the activist who gardens, the entrepreneur who dances. These aren't luxuries or distractions from "real work." They're essential foundations for sustainable resilience.

At its heart, resilience isn't about returning to who we were before difficulty touched us. It's about evolving through our encounters with challenge. The bamboo that survives the storm doesn't forget the experience of bending; it incorporates that knowledge into its very being. In this way, resilience becomes not just a response to difficulty but a continuous dialogue with life itself. Each challenge offers its particular wisdom; each recovery contains the seeds of the next transformation. We don't just survive our difficulties; we are remade by them, again and again.

> *At its heart, resilience isn't about returning to who we were before difficulty touched us. It's about evolving through our encounters with challenge.*

When I consider my path, I recognize how each period of uncertainty ultimately created space for something new to emerge. The voice I lost as a singer became the voice I found as an advocate. The stability I surrendered became the flexibility I needed to innovate. The comfortable identities I outgrew became doorways to more authentic self-expression. There's a humility to resilience, a recognition that we don't always know what form our strength will take until we're tested. There's also a profound hope in it—a trust that we contain within ourselves resources we haven't yet discovered, capacities that await the very difficulties that will call them forth.

Perhaps true resilience isn't about avoiding storms or standing unmoved in their midst. Perhaps it's about learning to dance with uncertainty, to find our balance in motion rather than stillness. Perhaps it's about trusting that our capacity to respond to life's challenges is as innate as the bamboo's ability to bend, a wisdom encoded in our very being, waiting to be remembered when we need it most.

This is the resilience our times demand, not just to survive uncertainty but to create meaning within it. Not just to endure difficulty but to be transformed by it. Not just to weather the storm but to become the shelter that others need.

In the words often attributed to Ernest Hemingway, "The world breaks everyone, and afterward, some are strong at the broken places." May we all find that strength, not despite our wounds but because of them. May we all become kintsugi souls, our fractures filled with gold, stronger and more beautiful for having been broken.

# PART 3
## OPENING WITH CARE

# BOUNDARIES

*defining where we end and others begin*

In our quest for connection and belonging, boundaries are sometimes seen as walls we put up to protect ourselves from other people. I see boundaries not as dividers but as the invisible architecture of our relationships. As sacred thresholds that define our personhood. They are the essential contours of identity that allow us to show up authentically, both for ourselves and for others.

And yet, when the world feels uncertain, our sense of boundary gets shaky. Sometimes we overextend, carrying more than is ours to hold. Other times, we shut down completely, mistaking numbness for strength. We bend toward what's expected, even as we lose track of what's real for us. In a brittle culture, boundaries can be dismissed as indulgences—as if protecting your energy were a luxury, not a prerequisite for sustainable care.

I've learned this the hard way. As a longtime advocate for equity, I thought constant availability was part of the job. I said yes more than I meant it. I stayed up late answering "just one more email." I convinced myself it was commitment, not depletion.

But depletion has a cost. It isn't just about feeling tired. It's about losing access to yourself. And when that happens, the work you're trying so hard to serve starts to suffer, too. When we fail to set boundaries, we risk losing the clarity and presence that make our contributions meaningful.

What I've come to understand is this: boundaries aren't barriers to generosity—they're what make generosity real. When I say, "this is what I can give," I'm not withholding. I'm anchoring. I'm creating the conditions for something sustainable. And when I say, "this is where I end," I'm making space for others to meet me, not as dependents, but as whole people in their own right.

> *Boundaries aren't barriers to generosity—they're what make generosity real.*

It's a paradox. Boundaries protect us, yes. But they also protect the relationship. They allow it to be honest. Mutual. Alive. Because without them, something essential breaks down. We stop telling the truth about what we need. We overfunction. Or we vanish.

That's what I mean when I say boundaries are a form of truth-telling. They invite us into deeper honesty about what's working, what's not, and what we're available for. But that kind of honesty takes practice. It asks us to pay attention to our capacity. To learn its shape. To notice where it ends. And to name that with care.

This isn't easy work. Especially in times of stress, when the world demands more than we can possibly give. But that's when it becomes most important. That's when we most need to ask: What's essential here? And what am I carrying that doesn't belong to me?

I've seen this boundary erosion play out again and again inside organizations. You can feel it in the unspoken expectations, the pressure to be endlessly available, to absorb discomfort without naming it, to smile through what hurts. Especially for those from marginalized identities, the cost of these dynamics runs deep. They're often asked to carry the emotional weight of systems they didn't build, while being given no room to speak honestly about that weight.

I've watched brilliant colleagues slowly burn out, not because they lacked resilience, but because the culture demanded too much and returned too little. Emotional labor goes unacknowledged. Speaking up gets framed as troublemaking. And slowly, that invisible toll hollows people out.

We don't usually lead with our boundaries. Instead, we learn to bend, to accommodate what hasn't been said out loud. To anticipate. To soften our truth to fit what others can handle. It's praised as professionalism. Or being a team player. But often, it's something else: a slow erosion of self.

And the irony? That very erosion makes genuine connection impossible. Because when we disappear ourselves, we can't meet others fully. And they can't truly meet us.

That's why boundaries matter so deeply. They bring the unseen into the light. They give language to the things we've been feeling but haven't quite known how to say. They make visible the forces that quietly shape our choices, and in doing so, they open the door to something more honest.

And still, it's not easy. There's pain in this practice. When we begin to draw boundaries after years of silence or overextension, things shift. People push back. Dynamics change. Some relationships need to be renegotiated. Some may not survive. There's grief in that. But there's also clarity. And, eventually, relief.

What I've learned is that setting boundaries doesn't mean shutting others out. It means coming back to myself so that I can show up more fully. It's not about choosing between my needs and someone else's. It's about honoring the space where both truths can exist, even if they're in tension.

> *Setting boundaries doesn't mean shutting others out. It means coming back to ourselves, so that we can show up more fully.*

That space where honesty and compassion meet is where something new becomes possible, not just for us, but for the people around us.

Boundaries, when practiced with intention, create a kind of quiet power. A clarity. I've seen it in small moments, like when someone apologizes for being direct in a challenging conversation, then pauses and says, "But this is still my truth." That moment, right there, is a turning point. It shifts something. Having the honesty and courage to endure discomfort does more than smooth conflict; it builds trust.

There's something profoundly freeing in letting go of the performance of composure. In allowing your authentic voice, not your polished one, to come through. It's in those moments, the ones that might feel messy or even a little risky, that relationships start to feel real.

And the more chaotic the world feels, the more necessary this becomes. In a brittle, anxious, nonlinear, incomprehensible world, boundaries are what keep us grounded. They remind us where we stand. They let us navigate without losing ourselves.

Because here's the truth: without boundaries, our capacity frays. Our presence thins. Our impact dims. But with them? We're able to stay in the work. To show up again tomorrow, and the day after that, because we are trading depletion for alignment.

> *Without boundaries, our capacity frays. Our presence thins. Our impact dims.*

This isn't selfishness. It's devotion. Devotion to the work, to the people we serve, to the integrity of our own being. Boundaries protect not just our time or energy, but our ability to offer something real.

So the questions become: Where am I being asked to overextend? Where have I gone quiet about my limits? And what needs to be reclaimed so I can give from a place that's whole, not hollowed out?

There are no formulas for this. No perfect scripts. The answers will come slowly—through quiet listening, through honest conversations, through daily practices that bring us back to ourselves.

Because connection that matters, the kind that endures, only happens when we know where we end and where we begin. That's when real relationship becomes possible. Not from performance. Not from obligation. But from truth.

# VULNERABILITY

*Risking authentic connection*

There's an image that comes to mind when I think about my journey with vulnerability. I'm standing on a stage, preparing to give a talk—not just any talk, but one that would require me to reveal something I had kept hidden for years. I had spent years avoiding this story. It was too raw, too personal, and frankly, too painful. Yet there I was, about to share it with hundreds of strangers.

The vulnerability of that moment felt like standing at the edge of a cliff, the drop both terrifying and somehow necessary.

The word "vulnerability" comes from the Latin *vulnerare*, meaning "to wound." To be vulnerable is to risk being wounded. Only through this willingness to risk pain can we create the conditions for genuine connection.

> *Only through the willingness to risk pain can we create the conditions for genuine connection.*

Yet, for many of us, particularly in professional settings, vulnerability feels counterintuitive. We've inherited notions of leaders as impenetrable fortresses—people who have the answers, who show no weakness, who remain stoic in the face of challenges.

But true vulnerability transcends judgment. It acknowledges fear and uncertainty and shows up anyway. It is the courage to be seen, fully and honestly, with all our imperfections intact. Not as a performance, but as a human offering.

I often use the metaphor of an iceberg when talking about identity and disclosure in professional settings. Above the waterline are aspects of ourselves that are visible or that we readily share: our job titles, our education, perhaps aspects of our appearance or identity that cannot be hidden.

But below that waterline lies so much more: our struggles, our fears, our deepest values, aspects of our identity that carry stigma in certain contexts, the stories that have shaped us.

The decision about what to bring above the waterline—what to disclose, when, and to whom—is deeply personal. It involves real calculations about safety, about potential consequences, about psychological readiness. There is no universal "right amount" of vulnerability that works for everyone in every context.

But I have witnessed, again and again, the power of lowering that waterline, even incrementally. When we share something authentic about ourselves, particularly something that might carry stigma or has been difficult to navigate, we create a ripple effect that extends far beyond that single act of courage.

And now we know something more: vulnerability is not just personal courage, it is cultural design.

Through his research, Tim Clark, a leading expert on psychological safety, identifies just two mechanisms responsible for shaping team norms and building psychological safety:

1. Modeling vulnerability yourself
2. Rewarding the vulnerability of others

That's it. Those are the levers.

"How well or poorly we do this determines the norms on a team," Tim explains. "We can't find any other mechanism for culture formation." The implications are profound. If you're a leader, you are constantly shaping culture. There's no off switch. You can't delegate that responsibility. You are either leading the way or getting in the way.

Even silence is significant. "If I am vulnerable to you and you don't respond, that's not nothing. A non-response is interpreted as negative."

This means vulnerability isn't optional. It's foundational. How we respond to one another's risk-taking—whether with presence or avoidance, with encouragement or withdrawal—sets the tone for everything that follows.

> *Vulnerability isn't optional.*
> *It's foundational.*

I've witnessed transformative moments when leaders step forward and share their struggles with bias, with understanding different experiences, with failing, learning, and growing. Far from diminishing their authority, this kind of openness humanizes them. It signals to others that they, too, can bring their whole selves into the space. It shifts vulnerability from an individual act to a collective possibility, where authenticity becomes the foundation of trust rather than its undoing.

This is the power of what Brené Brown calls "daring greatly," not perfect performances of invulnerability, but the messy, imperfect, beautiful courage to show up as we are.

Our cultural narratives often position strength and vulnerability as opposites: you can be strong or you can be vulnerable, but not both. This binary thinking is particularly

# Vulnerability

harmful in leadership contexts, where appearing strong at all costs becomes the default, even when it undermines authenticity and connection.

But what if true strength includes the capacity for vulnerability? The soft/strong binary collapses when you meet a leader who can say, "I don't have all the answers. I'm learning too. I'm willing to be changed by what I learn from you."

Consider the leader who admits uncertainty during a time of crisis, who shares their journey of learning and evolving on matters of inclusion, and who acknowledges missteps and commits to growth. This leader isn't displaying weakness; they're demonstrating the profound strength required to be human in front of others.

When we talk about vulnerability, we often focus on its risks: the risk of judgment, of rejection, of not being understood. These risks are real and should not be minimized, particularly for those whose identities already make them targets of bias or exclusion.

But there's another risk we talk about less often: the risk of not being vulnerable. Of keeping ourselves so tightly armored that no one, not even those closest to us, can truly see or know us. Of missing the connections that can only happen when we dare to be authentic. Of living half-lives of curated performances rather than full expressions of ourselves.

I think about the impact of stories shared by pioneers like Tim Cook, who, despite his initial reluctance, came out as a gay CEO of one of the world's largest companies, Apple. His disclosure wasn't just a personal act; it created lifelines of possibility for countless others who suddenly could see a future where they might not have to hide aspects of themselves to succeed.

This is what it means to lead from vulnerability: to extend ourselves not just for personal relief, but for collective transformation. To let others see us, and in doing so, to help them see themselves more clearly, too.

One of the most important things we can do, whether as leaders, colleagues, friends, or community members, is to create containers where vulnerability feels possible—where people understand that authenticity will be met with respect rather than ridicule, with understanding rather than exploitation.

These containers don't just happen. They require intentional cultivation, clear norms, and consistent reinforcement. In organizations, this means creating spaces where learning is expected, where mistakes are understood as part of growth rather than evidence of failure, where genuine questions are welcomed rather than shamed. It means modeling the vulnerability we hope to see, not demanding it from others while remaining unwilling to practice it ourselves.

At its heart, vulnerability is about connection, about the profound human need to be seen, known, and accepted. It's about the courage to risk rejection in pursuit of belonging.

> *Vulnerability is about the courage to risk rejection, in pursuit of belonging.*

For all of us, regardless of our identities or positions, there's a fundamental question that plays beneath our interactions, one that psychologist John Gottman identifies as the foundation of all relationships: *Can I trust you with my inner world?*

When we practice vulnerability, when we share something authentic about our experiences, our values, our struggles,

# VULNERABILITY

our hopes, we're essentially asking that question: Can I trust you with this piece of who I am?

And when that vulnerability is met with acceptance, with understanding, with reciprocal openness, the foundation for true belonging is laid.

This is especially important in our fractured time, when polarization and division seem to grow ever sharper.

Vulnerability may be one of our most potent tools for bridging these divides, not because it erases differences or glosses over real conflicts, but because it reminds us of our shared humanity beneath those differences.

Even now, decades into my work, I still feel that flutter of anxiety before sharing certain aspects of my story. I still carefully calculate which spaces feel safe enough for full disclosure. I still worry, sometimes, about the professional consequences of being too open, too raw, too much myself.

But I've learned to recognize these fears not as warnings to retreat but as signposts pointing toward growth, toward the edges where my comfort ends and the possibility of deeper connection begins.

In a world where so much feels uncertain, where so many of our institutions and assumptions are being questioned, vulnerability offers us a path forward, not because it gives us certainty, but because it gives us connection. Not because it makes us invulnerable to pain, but because it reminds us we're not alone in that pain.

Perhaps, in the end, vulnerability isn't about risking wounding at all. Perhaps it's about recognizing that we are already wounded—all of us, in different ways—and finding the courage to show those wounds to each other, to tend them together, to heal not in isolation but in community.

This is the invitation vulnerability offers us: to step out from behind our carefully constructed personas, to lower the waterline, to risk being seen, not just for who we wish we were, but for who we truly are. With all our beautiful complexity. With all our imperfect humanity. With all the courage it takes to stand at that cliff edge and jump, trusting that somewhere below, connection awaits.

# GRACE

*extending compassion to self and others*

So much of the cultural conversation around justice, equity, and inclusion has become marked by exhaustion, defensiveness, and deepening division. On all sides, people are walking away feeling misunderstood, mischaracterized, or simply worn down. The work of building more just organizations and communities, while vitally important, has come to feel, for many, like a battlefield rather than a bridge.

What's needed in this moment is an age-old human quality that's been largely missing from our public and professional dialogues: grace.

Grace, with all its layered meanings—from divine assistance to human elegance to the willingness to extend mercy—isn't just a spiritual idea or poetic sentiment. It's a practical and powerful force. One that can soften our defensiveness without diluting our values. One that makes space for both truth-telling and healing.

Those who've been leading efforts for justice, advocates working to call out inequities and shift power dynamics, have brought tremendous grit, courage, and clarity to the work. But many feel unseen. Dismissed. Misunderstood. The emotional and energetic toll of this labor is real.

Those who've been skeptical or critical of this movement, often people in positions of historical privilege, aren't always operating from bad faith either. Many feel unfairly judged or prematurely labeled. They too feel unseen.

We need to bridge these differences. We need to meet the deeper human needs that are surfacing in this moment. One way to do that is by practicing grace.

Grace is not the same as passivity. It does not excuse harm or erase accountability. What it does is create the possibility for repair. It makes room for humanity, in all its messiness, to stay at the table.

> *Grace creates the possibility for repair.*

Interestingly, grace has already had a quiet presence in our collective vocabulary. We speak of people "falling from grace", especially those in power who make public missteps. But what if we reframed the challenge of building more just workplaces as an invitation to fall into grace instead?

What if, instead of rushing to cancel someone who stumbles in their language or actions, we began by extending grace? What if the response to a misstep were not immediate shaming, but an invitation to learn, to reflect, and to return with greater awareness?

What if, instead of dismissing advocates for equity as angry or militant, those in dominant groups extended grace? Grace to those who are angry not because they hate, but because they care. Grace that recognizes righteous rage as a sign of someone's deep investment in justice, not their deficiency.

To give each other grace is to recognize our shared humanity. To empathize. To trust in each other's essential goodness.

For some, it may even be to recognize the divine spark that lives in each person, no matter how flawed.

This reframing of grace doesn't mean lowering standards. It doesn't mean tolerating abuse or harm. And it doesn't mean ignoring the very real systems of oppression we are working to change. Grace simply means we hold space for complexity. We understand that growth is rarely linear and that transformation often involves stumbling, apologizing, and trying again.

During my journey of evolving as a leader, advocate, and human being, I've come to understand grace not as a destination but as a practice we return to again and again. Grace is what allows us to acknowledge our humanity—with all its contradictions and unfinished edges—and to extend that same generous acceptance to others.

When I reflect on my own path, I recall conversations with leaders who believed they had to have all the answers. There was a misguided notion that vulnerability diminished authority. But what I've witnessed time and time again is that grace creates the opposite effect. It creates space for authenticity, for connection, for mutual respect. When leaders extend grace to themselves and others, they model strength through softness.

> **When leaders extend grace to themselves and others, they model strength through softness.**

One of the most profound gifts of grace is that it allows transformation to take root. Without grace, we stay locked in patterns of judgment and fear. We leave no room for the messiness of growth. We create cultures that are brittle instead of bold.

And we forget. We often forget how many times grace has been extended to us. How many people allowed us space not to know, to fumble, to begin again. Yet we are often far less generous with others who are now on *their* learning edge. In today's call-out culture, one mistake can result in total dismissal. This brittleness fractures connection and undermines the very transformation we're seeking.

This cultural impatience shows up not only in our relationships but also in our expectations about change itself. Grace asks us to move at a different pace. In a culture obsessed with speed, perfection, and immediate results, grace reminds us that profound change, personal or systemic, takes time. Not passivity. Not procrastination. But patience.

In the context of equity and justice work, grace reminds us that we're not all starting from the same place. Some of us have lived these realities for a lifetime. Others are waking up to them only now. Grace doesn't mean accepting harm or injustice, but it does mean accepting that people grow at different speeds, and that shaming rarely accelerates learning.

We also need grace when we are depleted. When the weight of advocacy, or leadership, or simply living through this moment becomes too much. Grace becomes essential for sustainability. It allows us to rest, to reset, and to return. It is the counterbalance to burnout.

So what might it look like to practice grace more intentionally?

It might begin with our internal dialogue, the way we speak to ourselves in moments of failure or disappointment. Grace invites us to meet our inner critic with compassion.

It might show up in how we respond to setbacks in our work, such as when a project doesn't go as planned, progress stalls, or tensions rise. Grace says, "This moment is hard, and it doesn't define the whole journey."

It might emerge in how we see others: not as defined by their worst moments, but as whole, complex beings capable of learning, growing, and doing better.

I've learned that grace is closely tied to humility. It requires acknowledging that we don't have all the answers. That we're not meant to do it all, know it all, or fix it all. We do what we can, with the gifts we have, and trust that others are doing the same.

Grace stands in contrast to perfectionism and panic. It reminds us that even amid uncertainty, we can choose how we relate to ourselves and each other. It creates a more spacious container for our humanity, one that holds both courage and compassion.

In extending grace, we create the conditions for true belonging. We make it safer for people to bring their whole selves, to take risks, speak honestly, make mistakes, and learn from them. Grace doesn't diminish accountability; it makes accountability possible.

Most importantly, grace reconnects us to our shared humanity. In a world that often divides and dehumanizes, grace insists on seeing the person before the position. The heart before the headline. It asks us to lead with empathy, even when we're angry. To stay in relationship, even when we disagree.

> *Grace insists on seeing the person before the position. The heart before the headline.*

This is the heart of what grace offers, not as a spiritual abstraction, but as a social technology. As a strategy for repair. As a path toward justice that doesn't require sacrificing kindness.

Where might you extend more grace to yourself or to others? Where might you receive grace, rather than resist it? What would it look like to build cultures where grace is not a weakness, but a strength?

The practice of grace is not about lowering our standards or accepting the status quo. It's about creating the psychological safety and human connection necessary for real transformation. When we lead with grace, we acknowledge both the difficulty of the path and the dignity of those walking it.

In the end, grace may be one of our most powerful tools for navigating uncertain times. It reminds us that even when we don't have all the answers, we can still show up with an open heart. Even when the way forward isn't clear, we can walk it together, with compassion and courage.

# KINDNESS

### *choosing to care*

When I examine the core of what has kept me going through my most difficult moments, through long stretches of advocacy work that felt like pushing a boulder uphill, it's the profound simplicity of kindness that emerges as the most transformative force in my life.

Kindness is both revolutionary and so utterly fundamental to our humanity.

Yet it's often the first casualty in times of stress and fear. When we're anxious, uncertain, or feeling protective of ourselves, our instinct is to contract, to create distance, to harden, precisely when the greatest healing could come from opening, connecting, and softening.

> *Kindness is often the first casualty in times of stress and fear.*

I believe kindness is both a practice and a perspective. As a practice, it asks us to take concrete actions: to listen deeply, to speak with care, to consider impact alongside intention.

## The Shape of Change

As a perspective, it invites us to see the world through a lens of shared vulnerability and interdependence.

The kindness I'm speaking of doesn't ask us to be perfect. It doesn't demand that we have all the answers or that we never falter. Instead, it invites us to bring our full, messy humanity to each interaction, to each decision. It asks us to care not because we know the outcome will be positive, but because caring itself is a form of resistance against the dehumanizing forces of our time.

Kindness asks us to hold complexity. It requires us to acknowledge that we can feel frustration, anger, and disappointment while still choosing to engage with care. It reminds us that we can fight passionately for our justice without dehumanizing those who stand in opposition. It suggests that the strongest position is not one of rigid certainty but of compassionate flexibility.

> *We can fight passionately for our justice without dehumanizing those who stand in opposition.*

For those of us engaged in efforts toward greater equality and inclusion, kindness has another dimension. It becomes a demonstration of our most deeply held values. A living testimony to the belief that every person deserves dignity and respect regardless of their identity, background, or beliefs.

Kindness acknowledges the uniqueness of each person's journey and asks us to meet people where they are, not where we expect them to be. And that includes ourselves. How often in the pursuit of justice and progress do we drive ourselves to exhaustion, become our own harshest critics, and neglect our bodies, hearts, and spirits?

## Kindness

This is where kindness becomes a radical act of self-preservation. It means establishing boundaries that protect our energy. It means forgiving ourselves when we fall short of our own ideals. It means recognizing when we need to step back, rest, and replenish so that we can return to the work with renewed clarity and purpose.

As leaders, our fundamental challenge is to cultivate this orientation toward kindness even—especially—in moments when it feels most difficult. When we're being criticized or misunderstood. When someone has disappointed or betrayed our trust. When institutional resistance makes progress feel impossible. Those are precisely the moments when our capacity for kindness becomes most transformative.

I want to be clear: this isn't about spiritual bypassing or toxic positivity. It isn't about ignoring harm or papering over genuine conflict with superficial niceness. The kindness I'm describing exists in dynamic tension with truth-telling and accountability.

Genuine kindness requires discernment. It means understanding when gentle support is needed and when firm boundaries must be established. It means recognizing that sometimes the kindest thing we can do is to name harmful behaviors directly rather than allowing them to continue unchallenged.

This is where the nuance of "calling in" versus "calling out" becomes so relevant. The key differentiator between these approaches is kindness and respect. Calling in requires pausing and choosing an approach that welcomes as much openness, reflection, and change in someone as possible, rather than seeking that momentary vindication that comes from shutting someone down or attacking them publicly.

Kindness is playing the long game. It requires tremendous discipline, patience, and truly, love and solidarity with other humans on their journey. As the saying goes, "We are all just walking each other home." Kindness acknowledges this shared pilgrimage.

> *If we are all just walking each other home, kindness acknowledges this shared pilgrimage.*

In the face of uncertainty, kindness grounds us in what is knowable: that human connection matters, that dignity is non-negotiable, that how we treat each other shapes the world we create together. It reminds us that even when we cannot control circumstances, we can control how we respond to them.

And responding with kindness, inevitably creates space for more kindness to emerge. My friend Julie Lythcott-Haims expresses this beautifully, "Kindness has this incredible ripple effect. If you are kind to me, overtly kind, in public, I will feel better because you've done a kind act for me. You will feel better because you've done something kind. Anyone watching will feel better because they've witnessed a kind act, and they are more likely to go out and do kind things for others."

This butterfly effect, this magical quality of kindness to replicate itself and expand outward, is precisely what makes it so powerful in times of uncertainty. When the ground feels unstable beneath us, acts of kindness become the handholds we reach for to steady ourselves. They're small acts of faith in our shared humanity, tiny rebellions against cynicism and fear.

The question isn't whether we can afford to be kind in uncertain times. The question is whether we can afford not to be. In a world where so much feels brittle and anxious, kindness offers a different way forward, not by denying the reality of our challenges, but by facing them with our full humanity intact while simultaneously committing to recognizing and honoring the full humanity of others. It asks us to pay careful attention to the wholeness of those around us, to see beyond roles and labels to the complex, multidimensional beings that we all are.

As we navigate these turbulent times, may we remember that kindness isn't just something we do when conditions are ideal. It's most needed, most powerful, most transformative precisely when conditions are not ideal—when we're scared, when we're hurting, when the future seems most opaque.

Kindness is the light we carry forward when the path is unclear. It doesn't illuminate the entire journey, but it shows us the next step. And often, that's enough.

> *Kindness is the light we carry forward when the path is unclear.*

# PART 4
## Relearning Connection

# RESONANCE

I've been thinking a lot about resonance lately, about how we don't just communicate with words, but with tone, with presence, with the space we create for others. Maya Angelou's words come to mind: People won't remember what you said or did, but they will remember how you made them feel. And isn't that the essence of tonality? It's not just about what we say, but how we say it—the way our voices carry, the way they land, the way they stay with people long after the moment has passed.

This resonance extends beyond voice alone. It's in how we hold space for another person, giving them our full attention in a distracted world. It's in the moment we pause to truly listen rather than simply waiting for our turn to speak. It's in how we make others feel significant by witnessing their truth with the same reverence we hope others will give to ours. So much of the work I've done with the *Will to Change* podcast has been about amplifying voices that aren't my own—not just being educated by them, but being fundamentally transformed by their resonance within me.

As a former musician and vocalist, I know that composers don't choose keys arbitrarily. Every note, every chord, every moment of tension and release is crafted to evoke something specific in the listener. Some sounds soothe; others provoke. And in our voices—whether spoken or sung—there's a frequency that can either draw people in or push them away.

But resonance isn't always about harmony. In fact, dissonance is often what makes music, and conversations, the most powerful. That moment of unresolved tension, of uncertainty, of discomfort—it's necessary. It keeps us engaged. It compels us to lean in, to listen more closely. And sometimes, in the work of transformation, that discomfort is precisely what's needed. We're not always meant to wrap things up in a neat bow. Sometimes we need to leave people with questions, with an ache, with the challenge to sit in the in-between.

> *Resonance isn't always about harmony.*

And often, the dissonance we create when speaking difficult truths precedes the most meaningful harmonies.

I think about this when I speak to audiences, lead teams, and hold space for hard conversations. We are all instruments in a way. Some moments call for us to step forward and claim the solo, to let our voices ring out with clarity and conviction. Other moments ask us to blend, to listen, to be part of something greater than ourselves. And the most skilled leaders, the ones who truly move people, know how to navigate between these roles with intention.

The irony of resonance is that the more specific and personal our truth becomes, the more universal its reach. We might fear that our particular story will alienate others, but I've found precisely the opposite. When we mine the most personal aspects of our experience, we often unearth the most universal human truths. The stories we're most afraid to tell often hold the greatest potential to create connection.

# Resonance

*The irony of resonance is that the more specific and personal our truth becomes, the more universal its reach.*

In the vulnerable place of speaking truth, our voices may crack; our words may stumble. We may sometimes strike the wrong note or lose the rhythm. But resonance doesn't require perfection. It asks us to show up with what is real, with what is true in this moment, even as we acknowledge that truth itself is constantly evolving.

In a world that often feels disconnected, speaking our truth becomes an act of profound connection. It's a way of saying, "Here I am, in all my complexity, in all my contradiction, in all my humanity." And in that revealing, we create the possibility for others to reveal themselves as well.

Resonance, at its heart, is an invitation. When we speak our truth with both courage and compassion, we invite others into a field of authenticity where genuine connection becomes possible. We create a space where others can feel safe enough to add their voice to the growing harmony.

The world doesn't need more noise. It needs more resonance. More voices speaking from that authentic center where personal truth meets universal experience. It needs your unique tone, your particular timbre, your distinctive melody. No one else can create the vibration that you can create.

*No one else can create the vibration that you can create.*

Think about an orchestra. Each instrument has its unique voice, its distinct contribution. A violin doesn't try to sound like a trumpet, nor does a flute aspire to be a cello. The beauty emerges from each instrument playing its authentic part while remaining in relationship with the whole.

Because at the end of the day, it's not just about volume. It's about vibration. It's about feeling. It's about the way our voices linger in the hearts and minds of those who hear them. And their voices linger in us, creating an ongoing dialogue that transcends the moment. This is how we create not just solos but symphonies—not by disappearing into sameness, but by bringing our authentic instruments into relationship with others. Together, we create a full orchestral sound of diverse voices that enables even greater resonance and more beauty than any of us could produce alone.

And if we can be mindful of that—if we can learn to tune ourselves to the frequency of connection—then maybe, just maybe, we'll create something that truly lasts.

# BRIDGING

*reaching across divides*

I've sat across from people I was taught to distrust. People whose politics, beliefs, or identities were framed as threats to my own. But in those conversations—awkward, tense, sometimes fumbling—I discovered something unexpected: not agreement, but humanity.

In our polarized world, we're increasingly sorting ourselves into camps, into bubbles of like-minded thinkers. The algorithms that power our digital lives reinforce this tendency, feeding us more of what we already believe. Meanwhile, the spaces between us grow wider, deeper, and more treacherous to cross.

Yet it is precisely in those spaces—in that challenging, uncomfortable terrain between established positions—where the most important work of leadership happens.

The bridge is a powerful metaphor for me. Bridges don't eliminate the chasms they span; they acknowledge them. They don't pretend the divide doesn't exist. Instead, they create a pathway across it while honoring its reality. The bridge says: yes, there is distance between us. And yes, we can still reach each other.

# The Shape of Change

> *The bridge says: yes, there is distance between us. And yes, we can still reach each other.*

When I think about what it means to bridge in today's world, I'm drawn to consider what makes a bridge strong enough to withstand the storms we face together.

A bridge's strength isn't in its rigidity but in its ability to flex. Engineers design bridges to move with the wind, to absorb the energy of earthquakes, and to expand and contract with temperature changes. Perhaps our capacity to bridge divides requires a similar flexibility, not of principle, but of approach. Not a compromise of values, but an expansion of understanding.

Building bridges across our divides requires what one might call "intellectual humility", being righteous without being self-righteous. It's possible to hold strong views and values without dismissing others who see things differently. We can be firmly rooted in our truth while still acknowledging that our perspective is inherently limited, that there are always things we cannot see from where we stand.

I've learned that bridging begins with genuine curiosity. Not the performative kind that waits impatiently for someone to finish speaking so we can respond, but the deep kind that seeks to understand before being understood. It's about listening to comprehend rather than listening to reply.

When we truly listen across divides, we often discover that the person on the other side is not the caricature we've imagined. There is nuance, complexity, and humanity there, just as there is in us. We find that seemingly opposing positions often share underlying values, even if they express them differently.

I've come to believe that one of the most radical acts of bridge-building is to resist the binary thinking that dominates our discourse. This either/or mentality—you're either with us or against us—leaves no room for the messy, beautiful complexity of human experience.

One of the most damaging binaries we've absorbed is the false equivalence between discomfort and danger, especially in the context of identity and dialogue.

Our cultural discourse has increasingly blurred the line between discomfort and danger. We've seen, particularly in progressive spaces, how discomfort has become weaponized and viewed as a form of violence in itself. This shift has profound implications for how we connect across differences.

When we equate someone's imperfect language, honest question, or different perspective with actual danger, we lose the grace necessary to hold each other as we mutually learn and grow. We become brittle with each other and self-righteous, forgetting that we are all students and beginners in some aspect of human understanding. If we view each other as dangerous when we're most often simply trying to find our imperfect way back to connection, we will never transcend the othering binaries that divide us.

Bridging requires us to make space for imperfection, not to excuse harm, but to distinguish between what's harmful and what's merely hard. Without that clarity, we can't hold the tension necessary for connection. We'll either retreat from discomfort or respond to it with force. Neither builds a bridge.

> *Bridging requires us to make space for imperfection, not to excuse harm, but to distinguish between what's harmful and what's merely hard.*

We see this binary trap in how we approach ourselves, too. Many of us fall into the trap of believing we must be this or that, fitting into a specific box or category. Yet we all live at intersections. We are all, in our own ways, bridges between worlds, identities, and experiences.

To be a bridge is to stand in what some call "liminal space", the threshold between what was and what will be. It is to hold space for possibility, for transformation. The bridge is not just a path from here to there; it's a place in itself, a vantage point from which we can see both shores differently. When we reconceptualize the bridge itself not as merely a pathway between two static positions, but as a third space with its own unique value and wisdom.

This third space, neither fully one position nor another, becomes a place of emergence, where new possibilities arise that couldn't exist in either original position. It's a space of both/and rather than either/or, of generative tension rather than forced resolution.

And here's what's most challenging about bridging work: it demands vulnerability. To build a bridge, we must be willing to take the first step onto uncertain ground. We must risk being misunderstood, rejected, or criticized from both sides. The bridge-builder often stands alone at first, in that space between established camps.

Yet in that vulnerable place lies tremendous power. When we stand in the middle and reach out in both directions, we create the possibility for others to join us. We make visible a path that wasn't there before.

I think about how, when we're standing on a bridge, we can feel it sway and move beneath our feet. That movement can be unsettling—we like solid ground. But perhaps that very sensation reminds us of something essential: connection requires flexibility. Bridging requires us to feel the motion, to adjust our stance, to move *with* rather than *against* the inevitable tensions.

## Bridging

In our organizations, in our communities, in our families—wherever divides exist—we need more bridge-builders. We need those willing to step away from the safety of their established position to create pathways of understanding. And here's what I've found most hopeful: the act of bridging creates more bridges. When we model this work, others see that it's possible. They may find the courage to build their own bridges.

This bridging work begins, as all meaningful change does, with how we engage with ourselves. How do we bridge the divides within our own hearts and minds? How do we reconcile our contradictions, honor our multiple identities, and acknowledge our growth and changes? By practicing this internal bridging, we develop the muscles needed for external bridging work.

The truth is, we don't bridge divides by pretending they don't exist or by trying to collapse them prematurely. We bridge them by acknowledging their reality, by respecting their complexity, and by committing to the ongoing work of connection despite—and sometimes because of—our differences.

In a world that increasingly pushes us apart, the simple act of reaching across a divide with curiosity, compassion, and courage becomes a revolutionary act. It's an affirmation that what connects us runs deeper than what separates us. That beneath the noise of diatribe lies the possibility of dialogue. That even across the widest chasms, we can build bridges strong enough to hold us all.

> *In a world that increasingly pushes us apart, the simple act of reaching across a divide with curiosity, compassion, and courage becomes a revolutionary act.*

# BELONGING

*creating spaces of inclusion*

We arrive in this world wired for connection. From our first breath, we seek the gaze that affirms we are seen, the touch that tells us we are held, the voice that says we matter. This longing to belong doesn't diminish as we grow. It simply takes new forms, weaving through every aspect of our lives, shaping how we show up in our communities, our workplaces, and our most intimate relationships.

Belonging is perhaps the most fundamental of human needs, yet in our increasingly fragmented world, true belonging has become elusive for many. We find ourselves in spaces where we can participate but not fully contribute, where we are tolerated but not celebrated, where we are present but not truly seen. We learn to navigate these spaces by compartmentalizing, by covering aspects of our identity, by making ourselves smaller or quieter or less disruptive. We convince ourselves this is enough: to be included, to be allowed in the room. But deep down, we know there is a difference between inclusion and belonging.

There's a particular irony in how often I've witnessed organizations proudly announce their cultures of belonging while maintaining systems that require people to cover who they truly are. The diversity statement on the website sits alongside unwritten rules about professionalism that penalize cultural expressions outside the dominant norm. The celebration of Pride Month coexists with subtle expectations that LGBTQ+ employees won't make others uncomfortable by being "too out." The commitment to racial equity coexists with promotion practices that reward those who assimilate to leadership styles defined by and for the majority culture.

These contradictions aren't always malicious; they often stem from an incomplete understanding of what belonging truly requires. We've become adept at the language of inclusion without fully reckoning with how our structures, practices, and unspoken expectations continue to demand conformity rather than celebrating authenticity. We've mastered the art of inviting diverse people to our table without considering that perhaps the table itself—how it's structured, who built it, what behaviors are rewarded at it—might be the very thing preventing true belonging.

> *We've mastered the art of inviting diverse people to our table without considering that perhaps the table itself might be the very thing preventing true belonging.*

I think of all the rooms I've entered throughout my life where I carefully calibrated what parts of myself to reveal. As a woman in predominantly male spaces. As a queer person in environments where heteronormativity was the unquestioned default. As someone navigating the complexities of multiple identities in a world that prefers simple categories. I became skilled at these calculations, such as how much of myself could I safely bring forward? What aspects needed to remain hidden to maintain acceptance? What would be the cost of complete authenticity, and was I willing to pay it?

The exhaustion of this constant calculation is something many of us know intimately but rarely name. We develop a sixth sense for the unwritten rules: which topics are too political for the workplace, which personal stories are acceptable to share, which parts of our cultural heritage, gender expression, or family structure might make others uncomfortable. This vigilance consumes enormous amounts of energy. Energy that could otherwise fuel creativity, connection, and meaningful contribution.

What I've observed over decades of working with organizations is how often leaders underestimate this cost. They wonder why engagement surveys show disconnection while failing to recognize how their cultures subtly signal to many that complete authenticity is risky. They create "belonging initiatives" that exist alongside evaluation systems that reward those who most closely resemble the existing leadership in style, approach, and background. They express frustration when certain groups remain underrepresented at senior levels while maintaining narrow definitions of "executive presence" that effectively require covering from anyone outside the dominant group.

True belonging isn't about finding places where we can fit in by making ourselves acceptable to others. It's about creating spaces where we can all show up in our fullness without fear, spaces where dignity is not something to be earned but recognized as inherent to our humanity. Where our unique perspectives aren't merely tolerated but understood as essential threads in a richer, more vibrant tapestry. Where we don't have to leave parts of ourselves at the door but can bring our whole, integrated selves across the threshold.

Creating such spaces requires more than good intentions or inclusive policies. It requires a fundamental willingness to examine the disconnect between what we say we value and what our systems reward. It means asking uncomfortable questions: Whose comfort are we prioritizing when we establish norms around communication, conflict, or collaboration? What assumptions about "the right way to be" are embedded in our criteria for success? Which expressions of identity do we celebrate and which do we subtly suppress?

> *Whose comfort are we prioritizing when we establish norms around communication, conflict, or collaboration?*

This examination isn't about blame or shame. It's about honest recognition that most of our institutions were designed by and for a relatively homogeneous group of people, not out of malice, but from the limited perspective any homogeneous group naturally has. The structures they created inevitably reflect their experiences, preferences, and blind spots. Acknowledging this isn't an indictment of individual intentions; it's simply a necessary starting point for meaningful change.

I've witnessed the profound difference when organizations move beyond superficial inclusion initiatives to this deeper work of systemic transformation. When they commit not just to diversifying who sits at the table but to reimagining the table itself. When they create spaces for honest conversation about the gap between stated values and lived experiences. When they're willing to be uncomfortable, make mistakes, and learn continuously from perspectives they previously overlooked.

In these spaces, something remarkable begins to happen. People stop spending energy managing impressions and start investing it in genuine connection and creativity. They bring their full intelligence—not just the analytical kind but the emotional and intuitive kinds as well—to solving problems and generating new possibilities. They build relationships based not on superficial similarities but on authentic sharing across differences. And as a result, they discover capacities for innovation, adaptation, and meaningful work that were simply unavailable when everyone was trying to fit into a predefined mold.

But let me be clear: creating cultures of belonging isn't just good for organizations or communities in some utilitarian sense. It's fundamentally about honoring the dignity inherent in each human being. It's about recognizing that when anyone feels they must diminish themselves to be accepted, something essential is lost, not just for that person but for all of us. Each time someone cannot bring their whole self into a space, we all miss out on gifts that might have been shared, insights that might have been offered, and connections that might have been formed.

This loss is especially acute in times of uncertainty and change. When we face challenges that have no precedent, when we navigate terrain for which we have no maps, we need the full spectrum of human experience and perspective available to us. We need people who think differently, who see what others miss, who bring varied lived experiences to the questions before us. Yet these are precisely the moments when the pressure to conform, to cover, to present only the most acceptable parts of ourselves often intensifies.

> *When we face challenges that have no precedent, when we navigate terrain for which we have no maps, we need the full spectrum of human experience and perspective available to us.*

What would it mean to move through the world with an awareness of these dynamics? To enter each space, whether a meeting room, a classroom, a community gathering, or a family dinner, to notice not just the spoken values around belonging but the unspoken signals about who truly belongs? It would mean developing a new kind of attention, one that observes the gap between what we claim to value and what our practices reward. Who speaks and who remains silent. Whose ideas are built upon and whose are overlooked. Whose comfort is prioritized and whose is compromised.

It would mean cultivating the courage to address these contradictions, not with defensiveness or denial, but with genuine curiosity and commitment to change. To recognize that creating cultures of belonging requires more than good intentions or beautiful language. It requires the willingness to reimagine systems, to redistribute power, to reconsider what we've always taken for granted about how things are done. To understand that our intent, however noble, doesn't negate the impact of our actions or the structures we maintain.

And perhaps most challenging, it would mean embracing the vulnerability inherent in acknowledging that our organizations, and we ourselves, may be participating in the very dynamics we claim to be dismantling. That despite our best intentions, we may be asking people to cover in ways we don't even recognize. That our own comfort with the familiar may be limiting our ability to create spaces where others can truly belong.

I've experienced both sides of this equation: being the person required to cover essential parts of myself to be accepted, and being the person whose unexamined preferences or assumptions contributed to others feeling they couldn't fully belong. Neither role is comfortable to acknowledge. But I've found that this discomfort is precisely where the possibility of transformation begins. When we can hold both our genuine desire for inclusive communities and our participation in systems that undermine that desire, we open space for authentic change.

I believe this tension between our aspiration for belonging and the reality of our structures is not a reason for despair but an invitation to deeper work. Not an indication of failure but a natural part of the messy, imperfect process of human community evolving toward greater wholeness. What matters is not whether we've achieved perfect alignment between our values and our systems, but whether we're willing to continuously examine the gap and take meaningful steps to narrow it.

In the end, belonging isn't something we find; it's something we create together, moment by moment, choice by choice, relationship by relationship. It emerges when we dare to show up authentically and to create conditions where others can do the same. When we recognize that safety doesn't come from controlling what's allowed to be expressed, but from creating cultures where every expression is received with respect and care. When we understand that we don't need to be the same to belong to one another, we need only to recognize the dignity that lives in each of us and to commit ourselves to honoring it.

# Belonging

*In the end, belonging
isn't something we find;
it's something we create together.*

This is the work before us in these uncertain times: to move beyond the rhetoric of belonging to the reality of creating spaces where covering is no longer the price of acceptance. To recognize the contradiction between claiming to value authenticity while maintaining systems that penalize it. To have the courage to examine not just our intentions but the actual experience of those we invite into our communities. And from that honest examination, to begin the patient, imperfect work of aligning what we say with what we do.

May we find the courage for this journey. May we embrace the discomfort it inevitably brings. And may we discover, through our commitment to authentic belonging, not just healthier organizations and communities, but a more whole and human way of being together in this beautiful, broken world.

# CONNECTION

*fostering meaningful relationships*

Connection has become the resource we most desperately need yet struggle to cultivate. We've been sold a counterfeit version of connection that relies on the metrics of followers and likes, while the genuine article slips through our fingers. The cost of this substitution isn't merely personal discontent; it's visible in organizational dysfunction, societal polarization, and a collective hunger for something…more.

This crisis of meaning isn't new. It's the result of a long unraveling of wisdom that once kept us tethered to each other and the earth. In our rush toward technological progress, we've severed ourselves from connection systems that sustained humanity for millennia. The wisdom of elders, the grounding presence of natural cycles, the ritual practices that bound communities together—these weren't primitive stand-ins awaiting digital improvement, but sophisticated technologies of belonging we've hastily discarded.

What if our most innovative path forward actually involves reclaiming what we've forgotten? Indigenous cultures across the globe maintained profound practices for sustaining connection across differences, resolving conflicts, and making decisions that considered impacts seven generations ahead. These weren't early drafts of real connection but time-tested human technologies we've dismissed in our worship of the new.

The brutal truth? Most of what passes for connection in our professional lives is performance rather than presence. We've become adept at appearing engaged while guarding our authentic selves. We like, we follow, we engage, we comment, but we've forgotten how to sit in circles, how to listen to stories carried across generations, how to recognize ourselves as part of something larger and older than our individual ambitions.

> *Most of what passes for connection in our professional lives is performance rather than presence.*

This false dichotomy between professional effectiveness and authentic connection isn't just outdated, it's dangerous. Evidence increasingly shows that our capacity for meaningful connection directly supports resilience, innovation, and sustainable performance. Yet our leadership models and institutional structures continue to treat connection as a nice-to-have, a soft feature rather than a core function.

The deeper crisis lies in how we've severed connection from its roots. Connection isn't a technique to be mastered or a strategy to be deployed; it's the fundamental fabric of human experience. We've built workplaces, digital platforms, and social systems that actively obstruct the very thing we need most, while cutting ourselves off from the natural world that once served as our teacher, our mentor, our wise guide.

Real connection demands uncomfortable truths: that we are interdependent rather than self-sufficient; that vulnerability creates strength rather than diminishes it; that we cannot fully know ourselves outside the context of relationship. These truths challenge the individualistic, competitive narratives that dominate professional cultures. But they echo what our ancestors knew intimately: humans are not isolated entities but nodes in a vast, reciprocal web of life that includes not just each other, but the more-than-human world.

If our current systems devalue connection, what might it look like to design with connection at the center? The path forward requires dismantling the artificial boundary between our professional and personal selves, not by eliminating healthy boundaries, but by remembering that our humanity does not pause at the workplace door. It means recognizing that our ancestors—across traditions—developed rich technologies of connection that we abandoned not because they failed, but because they couldn't be monetized or scaled.

> *Connection isn't a technique to be mastered or a strategy to be deployed; it's the fundamental fabric of human experience.*

This isn't about superficial team-building exercises or mandatory socials. It's about creating spaces where people can show up fully human with their doubt, creativity, grief, and genius intact. It means challenging the assumption that professionalism requires emotional detachment. It means risking being known, not just recognized. And it means turning to wisdom traditions that understood connection not as a tool for productivity, but as the foundation of human flourishing.

## Connection

What might it mean to bring wisdom circles into board meetings? To honor the wisdom of organizational elders rather than shuffling them quietly toward retirement? To recognize that the natural world—with its seasons of rest, growth, renewal, and letting go—offers us a more sustainable model for human systems than our relentless drive for extraction and expansion?

> *The natural world—with its seasons of rest, growth, renewal, and letting go—offers us a more sustainable model for human systems than our relentless drive for extraction and expansion.*

This is a call. A challenge to reimagine how we gather, lead, and live. The organizations that survive the turbulence ahead will be those that recognize connection as their primary competitive advantage, not just in how they relate to customers or clients, but in the everyday quality of their internal relationships. Where connection exists, people bring greater creativity, trust, and courage to problems that would otherwise overwhelm them.

Connection in this sense becomes radical, a deliberate countercurrent to the dehumanizing pace and values of the digital age. It asks us to slow down when everything tells us to speed up. To listen deeply when skimming feels easier. To reveal our hearts when hiding feels safer. In many ways, it invites us to remember what our bodies have never forgotten: that we are wired for intimate, embodied connection in small, interdependent communities.

While this may all sound idealistic, it's also deeply pragmatic. The cost of disconnection is increasingly visible: burnout, turnover, disengagement, and innovation fatigue. What once felt like a soft concern has emerged as hard infrastructure. Our ancestors knew connection wasn't optional; it was survival. We are rediscovering this truth as our disconnection plays out in the breakdown of the systems we depend on.

The most urgent question for leaders is no longer how to optimize existing systems, but how to design environments where meaningful connection can take root. This requires examining our assumptions. Asking: What structures are holding connection back? Which inherited practices might need to be released to make room for something more humane, more enduring?

> *Which inherited practices might need to be released to make room for something more humane, more enduring?*

And perhaps the way forward isn't something new at all, but something ancient we are finally ready to remember. It means looking beyond the boundaries of modern organizational theory to practices passed down across generations from indigenous councils to seasonal rites of passage, from mentoring across generations to reciprocity with land and place. These aren't curiosities; they're our maps.

Our capacity for connection isn't diminished by the complexity of this moment; it's made more essential. In uncertainty, connection offers not just comfort but intelligence. It's a form of collective nervous system regulation, of remembering what matters, and of staying human together. The people, communities, and organizations who commit to it, deeply and deliberately, will be the ones most capable of moving through what lies ahead.

The rise of artificial intelligence adds new urgency to this task. We don't yet know whether AI will become a tool for deepening human connection or a force that fragments it further. But in the face of such uncertainty, our need for grounded community, shared meaning, and relational wisdom becomes even more essential.

The opportunity before us is to reclaim connection from the realm of corporate jargon and restore it to its rightful place as the foundation of meaningful human systems. It's about remembering that our longing for meaningful connection is not a distraction from real work but the very ground from which real work becomes possible.

This reclamation invites humility. It asks us to look backward, not out of nostalgia, but to retrieve wisdom we urgently need. Our ancestors knew how to stay connected across difference, how to hold conflict in community, how to pass on stories that carried identity and values. What might we learn from them that digital collaboration tools can't teach? What guidance might the rhythm of seasons offer that our always-on schedules obscure? What wisdom are we discarding when we send our elders quietly into retirement?

Connection, properly understood, isn't a separate function from performance, innovation, or resilience; it is the soil from which they all grow. When we recommit to authentic human connection as non-negotiable, we don't lose efficiency; we gain integrity. We gain aliveness. We create the conditions where people can thrive as whole human beings.

In a world fracturing along countless fault lines, the revolutionary act is to build bridges, not just of technology, but of care. Not just of collaboration, but of belonging. This work begins not with grand gestures, but with the daily practice of seeing and being seen, listening and being heard, remembering the sacredness in every person we meet.

Connection isn't just how we survive this moment; it's how we find meaning within it. It's through our relationships with each other, with our ancestors, with the natural world, that we remember who we are and imagine who we might become—together.

> *Connection isn't just how we survive this moment; it's how we find meaning within it.*

# PART 5
# Emerging, Again

# PURPOSE

## *finding meaning and direction*

There's this moment, maybe you've felt it, when everything you used to rely on just... disappears. Your title, your plan, even your sense of what you're good at. Gone. You find yourself standing in the middle of your own life, unsure which direction is forward. "What now?" becomes more than a question. It becomes the whole atmosphere.

I've been thinking about purpose lately; not as something we chase down like a job posting or a lightning strike, but as something quieter. Something that emerges when we're willing to sit still in the not-knowing, long enough to hear what's underneath the noise.

When the ground shifts and the familiar map burns up, we instinctively look for new coordinates. We want someone to hand us a clean "you are here" dot and a bold red arrow pointing to "next." But what if purpose doesn't work like that? What if it's not a destination at all, but a frequency we learn to tune into? A hum we notice when we're moving in alignment with something deeper than our roles, our résumés, or other people's expectations.

## The Shape of Change

> *When the ground shifts and*
> *the familiar map burns up,*
> *we instinctively look*
> *for new coordinates.*

I remember one of those moments a few years ago. The work I had poured myself into for decades, work that shaped my days and my sense of self, suddenly felt…complete. Not like I was done caring. Not like I was walking away. But like something inside me had landed. The book was out. The framework had taken root. The conversations were growing without me needing to push.

And with that completion came a strange kind of emptiness. Not grief. Not relief. Just space. Like a field after harvest: quiet, open, waiting.

Nobody really teaches us how to be in that space; we're expected to know. To have a five-year plan. A personal brand. A clever answer to what's next. But maybe genuine purpose, the kind that fits, only emerges when we stop trying to force it. When we let ourselves stand in the field, feel the wind, and pay attention to what wants to grow next.

I've come to believe that purpose isn't something we muscle into place through sheer will. It doesn't arrive on demand or take shape just because we're ready for it. It shows up in the tension between what we're good at and what the world quietly asks of us. Between what lights us up and what feels needed right now.

Sometimes it feels less like finding something and more like noticing. Noticing where there's an opening. A pull. A problem that won't leave us alone. A quiet invitation with our name on it.

## Purpose

My good friend Eduardo Placer often uses this quote in his storytelling coaching, and it feels particularly apropos here: "The story is hunting the storyteller."
But even when we sense it, we can't rush it. Purpose doesn't like being forced. It unfolds on its own timeline, like a seed that knows when to break the surface. All we can do is create the conditions: stillness, attention, a willingness to listen instead of push. And even then, it can feel like nothing's happening—until one day, something is.
That's where faith comes in. Not necessarily the religious kind, but the kind that helps you keep showing up. Faith that when everything else falls away, something essential will still be there. Faith that when you feel lost, the path is quietly forming under your feet.

*Purpose shows up in the tension between what we're good at and what the world quietly asks of us.*

Our culture is addicted to certainty. We celebrate people who sound like they've got it all figured out—vision, plan, timeline, pitch deck. But what if there's wisdom in the not-knowing? What if uncertainty isn't a detour, but the actual terrain?
Looking back, some of the most meaningful turns in my life happened during times of confusion and disorientation. When I lost my voice as a singer, I had no idea that loss would open the door to something new, a voice I didn't know I had, in a space where I didn't know I belonged. When I hit walls in organizational work, it forced me to ask deeper questions, not just about systems, but about humanity, about belonging.

## The Shape of Change

At the time, those moments felt like breakdowns. But they weren't detours from my purpose. They were the path. That was my purpose revealing itself, layer by layer, in ways I couldn't have strategized if I tried.

The old maps don't work anymore. The ones that told us how to build a life—stable jobs, clear career ladders, predictable roles—they've mostly crumbled. For a lot of us, those paths just don't exist. Or they don't fit.

In this seemingly chaotic landscape, purpose becomes not a fixed point but a practice of orientation. Not "this is my purpose forever," but "this is what feels purposeful now." Not "this is the meaning of my life" but "this is where I'm finding meaning today."

At first, that might sound destabilizing, like we're letting go of too much. But for me, it's been the opposite. Letting go of the pressure to know has been a kind of relief. When I stopped trying to define my one true purpose, I started to notice how purpose actually shows up. In unexpected places, in side doors, in the way I show up rather than in what job title I carry.

I started thinking of purpose less as a fixed point to reach and more like a direction to walk in. Not "I've found it," but "I'm moving in alignment." Not a static label, but a way of being.

That shift changed everything. It made purpose feel alive. Something that responds to who I'm becoming and to what the world is asking for. And it reminded me of something else: that purpose often makes more sense in hindsight. Looking back, I can see the thread that runs through even the messiest chapters. I can see how the hard parts weren't detours; they were part of the weaving.

> *The hard parts aren't detours;*
> *they are part of the weaving.*

And maybe most surprisingly, I've realized that purpose doesn't always speak in big moments or grand visions. Sometimes it's a whisper. A gut feeling. A sense of rightness when something clicks. A flicker of aliveness when I offer something that matters.

The trouble is, those whispers are easy to miss. We live in a world that shouts. A world that loves certainty, performance, and achievement. It's hard to hear what's real when everyone's broadcasting their best selves.

So I've learned to listen differently.

- What's pulling my attention, even when it doesn't make sense on paper?
- What do I keep circling back to?
- What sparks energy, not from fear, but from a weird kind of excitement?
- What do I do that feels like play, but ends up helping someone else?

I don't always have clear answers. But I'm learning to sit with the questions, and to trust that purpose has its own way of revealing itself, if I stay in the conversation.

Finding purpose in uncertain times asks something that sounds almost backwards: the courage to begin before we're sure. To take a step that feels meaningful, even if the path beyond it is still foggy. To say yes and figure it out later.

I've done that more times than I can count, shifting from performer to trainer, from DEI consultant to thought leader.

## The Shape of Change

Each pivot felt like a leap into something I wasn't quite ready for. I never had the whole picture, just a flicker of "this feels right." And it turns out, purpose didn't wait at the end of the road. It showed up as I walked it.

That kind of movement takes trust, not just in ourselves, but in the process. In whatever name we give to the larger wisdom that seems to nudge us forward. It means being willing to look like a beginner again. To admit we don't know. To figure it out as we go.

In the most challenging moments, when the ground feels like it's disappearing beneath us, this becomes our anchor. Not "What is my purpose?" but:

- What matters to me?
- What do I want to embody, even when no one's watching?
- What's one small contribution I can make to what I care about?

Sometimes purpose isn't some heroic calling. Sometimes it's about bringing extraordinary presence to ordinary moments. Listening fully. Holding space. Being there when it counts.

Maybe the real question isn't "what's my purpose?" Maybe it's "what is purpose asking of me now?"

How is it pulling me to grow, to connect, to offer something tangible, right here, in this moment?

That shift changes everything. Purpose stops being a prize we chase and becomes a relationship we tend. Not something we own, but something we participate in. Not a problem to solve, but a living conversation we're having with life itself.

## Purpose

*Purpose stops being a prize we chase and becomes a relationship we tend.*

And in uncertain times, when every map feels outdated and the way forward keeps changing, that conversation matters even more. Not because it gives us answers. But because it gives us orientation. Because it reminds us what we're made of. What we care about. What kind of world we're trying to build.

So instead of asking, "What should I do with my life?" maybe start smaller.

Ask:

- What's alive in me right now?
- What matters today?
- Where can I offer something of value, even if it's small?

And then, gently, honestly, courageously, follow where that leads. Knowing that purpose doesn't arrive all at once. It unfolds. It evolves. It walks with us—if we're willing to keep showing up, paying attention, and beginning again.

# POWER

*standing in truth and authority*

For too long, we've operated with distorted notions of power that leave us feeling either powerless or compelled to exert power over others. Both are manifestations of the same misunderstanding. Power isn't a zero-sum game where someone must lose for another to gain. Power, in its most authentic form, is generative; it creates more power.

> *Power, in its most authentic form, is generative; it creates more power.*

True power, the kind that transforms and elevates, comes from a fundamentally different place than power that dominates and controls. It emerges when we stand firmly in our truth and embrace the authority that only we can claim for ourselves.

My journey with power began with losing my voice—literally. As a trained opera singer, when vocal surgery derailed the career I'd worked toward my entire life, I experienced what felt like the ultimate powerlessness. The very instrument I'd cultivated to express myself was damaged, and with it, my future as I'd imagined it.

That loss forced me to reconsider where my power truly resided. Was it solely in my physical voice? Or was there something deeper that could never be taken from me: my perspective, my lived experience, my values, my capacity to witness and respond to the world around me?

So much of our power lives beneath the surface, under the waterline, as I often visualize it. These are the parts of ourselves we don't always share: the identities and experiences that have shaped us, the wisdom we've gathered through difficulty. Our power emerges when we bring these hidden parts of ourselves into the light, not by demanding that others recognize them, but by first acknowledging them ourselves.

For those of us with marginalized identities, this claiming can be revolutionary. We've been conditioned to hide parts of ourselves, to make ourselves smaller, to avoid making others uncomfortable with our difference. But what if we recognized that those very differences, those aspects of ourselves we've been taught to minimize, are actually the source of our unique power?

As our world becomes increasingly uncertain and divisive, finding and using our voice becomes even more crucial and more challenging. The noise is deafening. The pressure to conform is intense. The stakes seem impossibly high. But this is precisely when your unique voice matters most.

Standing in your truth requires the courage to be seen, really seen, for who you are. It means stepping onto the stage, sometimes literally, and sharing your perspective even when your voice shakes, when you aren't sure if you'll be welcomed, or you fear rejection.

It's not just performers or professional speakers who can access this kind of courage. Each of us has moments in our lives where we've stepped into uncertainty, taken risks, and spoken up even when it was difficult. These moments are the seeds of our power. But discovering courage is just the beginning. It's in wielding that courage consistently that we transform it into genuine power. When we exercise this courage repeatedly, it evolves into the power to convince, to persuade, to inspire, and to hold others accountable. It becomes the force that drives meaningful change, both within ourselves and in the world around us.

> *Wielding courage consistently transforms it into genuine power.*

If the thought of stepping onto that stage feels overwhelming, start smaller. Find a trusted friend or colleague and practice sharing a bit of your truth with them. Write your thoughts down, even if only for yourself. Record a voice memo that no one else will hear. The practice of articulating your perspective is itself a form of claiming your power.

Power is about being fully embodied, fully present, fully alive to the moment. It's about recognizing that leadership isn't something bestowed upon us by title or position; it's something we claim through our willingness to show up authentically and engage with the world around us.

When we foster connection and empathy within ourselves first, by acknowledging all the parts of who we are, listening to our inner wisdom, and honoring our needs and boundaries, we create a foundation from which authentic power can emerge.

Power also means recognizing that we all carry different constellations of privilege and marginalization. None of us is just one thing. I may be marginalized as a woman and as an LGBTQ+ person. Still, I also carry privilege as a white person, as someone with educational credentials, as someone who presents in ways that align with societal expectations in many contexts.

True power acknowledges both our strengths and our areas for growth. It doesn't pretend to know everything or have all the answers. Instead, it remains curious, open, and willing to learn.

> *Power doesn't pretend to know everything or have all the answers. Instead, it remains curious, open, and willing to learn.*

When I started my company, I didn't position myself as the expert. I recognized my strengths in building relationships and creating spaces for authentic conversation, and I hired individuals with deep expertise in diversity, equity, and inclusion work. I built the container, and then I invited in the experts who could help fill it with knowledge and wisdom.

Over time, as I listened and learned, I developed my own unique perspective. My power didn't come from knowing everything or claiming expertise I didn't have. It came from acknowledging what I did know, being transparent about what I didn't, and creating opportunities for collaboration that amplified everyone's strengths.

When I think about my journey to claim my power, I often return to the metaphor of being a messenger. I see my role as a conduit through which certain messages flow into the world. This framing helps me navigate the complexity of standing in my truth without falling into ego or self-importance. Yes, my perspective matters. Yes, my lived experience gives me insights that are valuable to share. But I'm also part of something much larger than myself—one voice in a chorus, one thread in a tapestry. And my devotion to my purpose is palpable.

Our power is amplified when we're in community with others who support and challenge us, who see us clearly and hold space for our growth. None of us claims our power in isolation. We need others who can reflect to us what they see, who can celebrate our strengths, who can gently point to our blind spots, who can remind us of our value when we forget.

> *None of us claims our power in isolation. We need others who can reflect to us what they see.*

In a world that's increasingly fragmented and polarized, building these communities of support becomes even more vital. They provide the ground from which we can stand firmly in our truth, the launching pad from which we can step into our authority.

Even in moments when we feel powerless—especially in those moments—we can remember that transformation is possible. That what appears to be an ending might actually be a beginning. That our power may be changing shape, evolving into something we haven't yet imagined.

Standing in your truth and claiming your authority doesn't mean having all the answers. It means being willing to ask the questions. It means staying present to the uncertainty. It means trusting that your voice—your unique, irreplaceable voice—is needed in this conversation about what it means to be human in these complex times.

# INTEGRATION

*bringing together all aspects of self and experience*

We live in a world that loves compartmentalization. We have our work self and our home self. Our professional identity and our personal story. The parts we show and the parts we keep hidden. The experiences that fit neatly into our narrative and those that feel like outliers, disruptions in the story we tell ourselves about who we are.

But what if the most potent form of leadership and the most authentic way of being comes not from this separation but from integration? From bringing together all the fragments, all the seemingly disparate parts of who we are and what we've lived?

Integration isn't about perfection. It isn't about having everything figured out or all the pieces neatly arranged. It's about the willingness to acknowledge all that we are: the light and the shadow, the certainty and the doubt, the strength and the vulnerability.

> *Integration isn't about perfection; it's about the willingness to acknowledge all that we are.*

There's a particular kind of courage required to say: This too is part of me. The experience that doesn't fit. The identity that seems at odds with another aspect of who I am. The failure alongside the success. The question living beside the answer. We often think of integration as a destination, a state of perfect alignment we'll someday reach if we just work hard enough, heal enough, grow enough. But what if integration is more like a practice, a daily commitment to showing up with all of who we are?

So much of our suffering stems from the illusion that we can separate the parts of ourselves, leaving certain aspects behind when we enter different spaces. We've been taught that this is professionalism, maturity, and what's expected. But at what cost?

When we fragment ourselves, we lose access to the very wisdom we need to navigate complexity. We cut ourselves off from the intuition that lives in our body, the perspective that comes from our lived experience, the empathy born from our wounds. In trying to present only our polished, perfect parts, we deny ourselves and others the gift of our wholeness. And in a BANI world, wholeness may be precisely what we need most.

> *When we fragment ourselves, we lose access to the very wisdom we need to navigate complexity.*

There's a feeling that comes with integration, a sense of resonance, of things coming into alignment not through force but through recognition. It's the feeling of "yes, this too" rather than "either/or." It's the release that comes from no longer holding parts of yourself at arm's length. I think

# INTEGRATION

of those moments when something I've kept separate, an experience, an identity, a question, suddenly finds its place in the larger constellation of who I am. Not because I've figured it all out, but because I've made room for it to exist alongside everything else.

These moments of integration often arrive unexpectedly. They come not when we're striving for some idealized version of ourselves, but when we surrender to what is. When we allow ourselves to be the complex, contradictory, beautiful mess that every human being truly is.

Integration invites us into a both/and world. Not either I am strong or I am vulnerable, but I contain both strength *and* vulnerability. Not either this experience defined me or it didn't matter, but this experience shaped me *and* I am more than any single moment of my life. This both/and thinking is essential in times of uncertainty. It allows us to hold multiple truths simultaneously. To acknowledge the reality of loss while remaining open to what might emerge. To honor what has been while creating space for what could be.

Integration doesn't ask us to resolve every tension or answer every question. It simply asks us to hold the tensions with awareness, to live the questions themselves, to allow apparent contradictions to exist within the larger ecosystem of who we are.

Perhaps the most beautiful thing about integration is that it's never complete. We are always becoming, continually encountering new, forgotten, or once-denied aspects of ourselves, constantly discovering new ways to unite what once felt separate. This unfinished quality isn't a flaw; it's the very essence of being human.

We are not static beings but dynamic systems, constantly in dialogue with ourselves and our world, continually renegotiating the relationship between our inner landscape and our outer expression. In embracing this ongoing process, we find a different kind of wholeness. Not the wholeness of completion, but the wholeness of acceptance.

In a world that pulls us in so many directions, that asks us to be one thing here and another there, integration becomes a radical act of reclamation. Of saying: I will not be divided against myself. I will bring all of who I am to what I do. I will allow all of my experiences—the joyful and the painful, the certain and the questioning—to inform how I move through this world.

> *Integration becomes a radical act of reclamation. Of saying: I will not be divided against myself.*

And in that integration, I just might find not only a more profound sense of personal wholeness, but a more authentic way of connecting with others, of creating spaces where everyone can bring their full humanity to the table.

# HOPE

*sustaining forward momentum with positive vision*

In the darkest moments of transformation, when we've surrendered to uncertainty and allowed ourselves to dissolve into that liminal space between what was and what will be, something remarkable begins to stir. Not certainty—we've released our grip on that illusion. Not answers—we've made peace with the questions. Something more elemental, more profound: hope.

Hope is perhaps the most misunderstood of human experiences. We often confuse it with optimism, with wishful thinking, with a naïve belief that everything will simply work out for the best. But true hope is made of sturdier stuff. It isn't built on denial of reality or avoidance of pain. It emerges precisely when we've had the courage to face what is, to feel it fully, to let it change us.

Hope lives in the space between acceptance and possibility. It whispers to us not "everything will be fine" but rather "something meaningful waits on the other side of this dissolution." It doesn't promise a particular outcome; it promises that our journey matters, that transformation has purpose, that what we're becoming has value even when we cannot yet see its form.

## The Shape of Change

I think of hope as a practice of radical imagination. Not fantasy, not escapism, but the soul's capacity to envision what might be born from the fertile soil of what is ending. It's the ability to sense the shape of emerging potential before it has fully materialized. To feel the energy of the new paradigm while standing in the rubble of the old.

> *Hope means to feel the energy of the new paradigm while standing in the rubble of the old.*

This kind of hope requires tremendous courage. It asks us to invest ourselves in possibilities we cannot prove, to orient ourselves toward a horizon we cannot yet clearly see. It demands that we remain open when every instinct screams for us to close, to contract, to protect what remains of the familiar.

There's a rhythm to hope that mirrors the natural world around us. Think of the forest after wildfire, seemingly destroyed, yet already containing within its charred landscape the seeds of its own renewal. Those seeds don't sprout immediately. They wait in darkness, gathering nutrients, building strength for the moment when conditions are right for emergence.

Our hope operates in similar cycles. There are seasons when it seems dormant, when the landscape of our lives appears barren. But beneath the surface, something essential is happening—integration, recalibration, gathering of resources. We're not failing when hope feels quiet. We're preparing for its next expression.

# Hope

> *We're not failing when hope*
> *feels quiet. We're preparing*
> *for its next expression.*

What sustains hope through these cycles? I've found it's rarely grand visions or sweeping rhetoric. It's the small moments of connection, of meaning, of beauty that remind us what it means to be fully human. A conversation where we feel truly seen. A moment of unexpected grace. A glimpse of someone embodying the values we aspire to live by. These moments are not distractions from our serious work of transformation; they are its lifeblood.

Hope is profoundly relational. While each of us must find our own relationship with possibility, we don't generate hope in isolation. We kindle it in one another, catching glimpses of potential through others' eyes when our own vision has dimmed. This is why creating spaces of authentic connection becomes so essential in times of great uncertainty. We don't just share information or strategies; we share the vital energy of possibility itself.

And yet, hope is not merely something we receive from others. It's something we actively cultivate within ourselves through our attention and practice. What we focus on grows. Where we direct our gaze shapes what we're capable of perceiving. This doesn't mean ignoring difficult realities, quite the opposite. It means looking directly at what is, while simultaneously remaining attuned to the subtle signals of what's emerging.

In the world we now inhabit, maintaining this quality of attention becomes both more challenging and more essential. When the pace of change accelerates beyond our capacity to make sense of it, when contradictory information bombards us from all sides, when even fundamental truths seem unstable, hope requires a different kind of grounding.

This grounding comes not from certainty about outcomes, but from clarity about values. Not from knowing what will happen, but from knowing what matters most to us, regardless of what happens. Not from having the right answers, but from asking the most life-giving questions.

I've found that in times of profound disorientation, hope lives in the questions themselves. Not the anxious questions that spiral into paralysis—What if everything falls apart? What if I'm not enough?—but the generative questions that open space for emergence: What wants to be born through this disruption? What deeper truth is being revealed? What if I'm being prepared for something I couldn't have imagined before?

> *In times of profound disorientation, hope lives in the questions themselves.*

These questions don't deny the reality of loss or the legitimacy of grief. They simply create a container large enough to hold both what is ending and what is beginning. They remind us that transformation is rarely a clean break from past to future, but rather a complex integration of what has been, what is, and what might be.

Perhaps this integration itself is the deepest source of hope. When we can hold the full spectrum of our experience—the grief and the possibility, the ending and the beginning, the known and the unknown—we discover a more resilient relationship with change itself. We become less brittle, less anxious in the face of non-linear, incomprehensible reality.

# Hope

We find ourselves capable of bending without breaking, of flowing without losing our essential nature.

This is not the hope of certainty, but the hope of capacity. Not "I know this will turn out well," but "I trust my ability to meet whatever comes with presence and integrity." Not "everything happens for a reason," but "I can create meaning from whatever happens."

The most powerful vision isn't one of a perfect future where all problems are solved and all wounds healed. It's a vision of ourselves and our communities moving through ongoing transformation with greater wisdom, compassion, and creativity. It's a vision of becoming ever more fully human together, even—perhaps especially—in the midst of circumstances we never would have chosen.

This is the sustaining power of hope: not that it promises an end to difficulty, but that it reveals the profound meaning available within difficulty itself. Not that it offers an escape from uncertainty, but that it shows us how uncertainty can become the doorway to deeper truth. Not that it gives us back control, but that it introduces us to a different kind of power altogether, the power that comes from aligning ourselves with life's inherent capacity for renewal and growth.

> *Hope doesn't promise an end to difficulty, but reveals the profound meaning available within difficulty itself.*

As our journey through these reflections comes to a close, I invite you to consider: What form is hope taking in your life right now? What questions are generating possibility for you? What values are providing orientation when certainty is nowhere to be found?

These questions have no right answers. They're invitations to a conversation that will unfold over time, in your unique way. But I believe that in the very asking, something essential is already happening. You're creating space for hope to find you. You're signaling your willingness to participate in the great becoming that is always underway, within you and around you.

In the end, hope isn't something we manufacture through positive thinking or force of will. It's something we attune ourselves to recognize, a frequency we learn to receive. It's already present amid everything that seems to contradict it: in the courage of those who stand for truth when it's unpopular, in the persistence of those who build community in fragmented times, in the creativity of those who imagine new possibilities where others see only dead ends.

And perhaps most importantly, hope is present in you. In your willingness to engage these reflections, to sit with the questions, to remain open to transformation even when it would be easier to close. That willingness itself is hope in action. It's the first green shoot pushing through charred earth. It's the whisper of what's possible when we have the courage to let go of who we've been so we can become what's needed next.

May you recognize the hope that lives within you. May you kindle it in others. And may we walk together into the uncertainty of these times not with false confidence, but with genuine trust in our collective capacity to become more fully human with each step we take.

# TO MY READERS

Thank you for reading *The Shape of Change*. This book reflects not just my professional journey, but a deeply personal one… the shedding, unlearning, and becoming that leadership asks of us today.

We are living through a threshold moment that demands more than incremental adjustments. The systems, structures, and ways of being that brought us here are inadequate for where we need to go. This isn't just about optimizing our leadership style or refining our organizations; it's about fundamental transformation. About allowing ourselves to dissolve and reform in service of something more human, more connected, more real in the face of fewer clear answers or the ability to anticipate what's next.

I wrote this book because I believe we are being called into a liminal space where everything is up for questioning: how we lead, how we relate, who we've been, and what kind of humans we need to become. This isn't comfortable work. It asks us to release our grip on certainty and step into the unknown together. But it's also the most important work of our time, and an urgent invitation for each of us, and organizations, to evolve.

If these pages sparked something in you—a recognition, a question, a stirring toward change—I hope you'll stay close. The conversation is just beginning, and we need each other for what comes next. Transformation has always been a collective endeavor.

With deep gratitude for your willingness to walk into uncertainty with courage, and always with grace,

Jennifer

# STAY IN THE CONVERSATION

You've read *The Shape of Change*, now let's shape what comes next, together.

This book is just the beginning. If my words resonated with you, if you saw yourself in the stories, the questions, or the quiet calls to courage, I'd love to stay connected.

## LISTEN IN

Every week on *The Will to Change*, I sit down with bold thinkers, everyday leaders, and visionaries to talk about what it means to lead with more humanity, at work and in the world. We cover everything from power and privilege to trust, grief, and the evolving nature of belonging. If you're craving honest, thoughtful conversation, I hope you'll join us. jenniferbrownspeaks.com/the-will-to-change.

## JOIN THE COMMUNITY

I'm building a more personal, more connected space for leaders, coaches, and curious humans who are walking this path with me. If you'd like to hear about new learning opportunities, live conversations, or coaching experiences inspired by *The Shape of Change*, this is the place.

Sign up at jenniferbrownspeaks.com/the-shape-of-change.

## Bring the Work Into Your Organization

I continue to keynote conferences, lead executive sessions, and support organizations that are ready to evolve. If you're planning an event, reimagining leadership, or deepening your commitment to culture change, I'd love to talk.

jenniferbrownspeaks.com/speaking
info@jenniferbrownspeaks.com

## Say Hello

I really do want to know what this book stirred in you. What landed? What questions are you holding now? I read your messages, and I'm always listening. Reach out directly at info@jenniferbrownspeaks.com.

## Spread the Word

If *The Shape of Change* moved you, I'd be honored if you shared it. Post a quote, tag @JenniferBrownSpeaks, or leave a review. You never know who needs the invitation next.

Together, we're building what's next. One conversation, one question, one brave act at a time.

# BRING ME TO YOUR ORGANIZATION OR EVENT

Over the years, I've had the privilege of speaking to leaders, teams, and change agents across the globe, from Fortune 100 boardrooms to grassroots leadership gatherings. No matter the setting, the most powerful conversations happen when we lean into discomfort, let go of perfection, and lead with more of ourselves.

As an internationally recognized and award-winning keynote speaker, I create experiences that are timely, human, and deeply relevant to the challenges leaders are facing today.

You can work with me in a variety of ways:

- Keynotes (in-person or virtual)
- Executive coaching and leadership circles
- Conversational design and team engagement strategy
- Custom sessions to deepen trust, clarity, and connection

Every engagement is tailored to your people, your culture, and your moment. I speak on themes such as:

- Human-centered leadership in times of disruption
- Building inclusive cultures and repairing trust
- The evolving nature of belonging at work

- Leading with courage, care, and emotional intelligence
- Supporting generational shifts and the future of leadership

If *The Shape of Change* sparked something for you and you're ready to bring this work into your organization, I'd love to connect. If you're feeling the nudge to bring this into your team, community, or event, reach out. I'd love to explore what's possible together.

Email: info@jenniferbrownspeaks.com
Website: jenniferbrownspeaks.com
LinkedIn: linkedin.com/in/jenniferbrownspeaks

# ABOUT THE AUTHOR

**Jennifer Brown** (she/her) is an award-winning speaker, bestselling author, and globally recognized authority on inclusive leadership and workplace culture. She's advised top organizations like Google, IBM, and the Gates Foundation, and is the author of How to Be an Inclusive Leader and Beyond Diversity. Her Inclusive Leader Continuum™ is used across industries to drive lasting change. Through her keynotes, podcast (The Will to Change), and advisory work, Jennifer helps leaders build cultures of belonging where everyone can thrive. She lives in New York with her partner of nearly 30 years, Michelle.

Learn more at www.jenniferbrownspeaks.com.

Made in United States
North Haven, CT
20 February 2026